Meaning and Representation

T0366504

Meaning and Reference

Meaning and Representation

Edited by

Emma Borg

Blackwell Publishers

© 2002 by Blackwell Publishers Ltd
a Blackwell Publishing company

First published as a special issue of *RATIO*, 2001

Editorial Offices:
108 Cowley Road, Oxford OX4 1 JF, UK
    Tel: +44(0)1865 791100
Osney Mead, Oxford OX2 0EL, UK
    Tel: +44(0)1865 206206
350 Main Street, Malden, MA 02148–5018, USA
    Tel: +1 781 388 8250
Iowa State University Press, a Blackwell Publishing company, 2121 S. State Avenue,
    Ames, Iowa 50014–8300, USA
    Tel: +1 515 292 0140
Blackwell Munksgaard, Nørre Søgade, 35, PO Box 2148, Copenhagen, DK-1016,
    Denmark
    Tel: +45 77 33 33 33
Blackwell Publishing Asia, 54 University Street, Carlton, Victoria 3053, Australia
    Tel: +61(0)3 347 0300
Blackwell Verlag, Kurfürstendamm 57, 10707 Berlin, Germany
    Tel: +49(0)30 32 79 060
Blackwell Publishing, 10, rue Casimir Delavigne, 75006 Paris, France
    Tel: +331 5310 3310

First published 2002 by Blackwell Publishers Ltd

Library of Congress Cataloguing-in-Publication Data has been applied for.

ISBN 0–631–23577–9

A catalogue record for this title is available from the British Library.

Set by Cambrian Typesetters Ltd.

For further information on
Blackwell Publishers visit our website:
www.blackwellpublishers.co.uk

CONTENTS

ANNOUNCEMENT

As this volume was going to press, the very sad news was announced of the death of Professor Gregory McCulloch. Greg was a lecturer in Philosophy at Oriel College, Oxford, the University of Leicester, and the University of Nottingham, before taking up a Chair at the University of Birmingham (a position he held from 1995 until his death). He was well known for his work in the philosophy of language, which included the classic introductory book *The Game of the Name*, and the philosophy of mind, including his 1995 book *The Mind and its World*. He was also interested in, and published on, Wittgenstein and existentialism. Shortly before his death, he finished work on a comprehensive presentation of his philosophical ideas, the *Life of the Mind* (to be published posthumously). He will be sorely missed.

CHAPTER 1

INTRODUCTION

The 2000 Ratio conference was on meaning and representation. The speakers were Tim Crane, Jerry Fodor, Paul Horwich, John Hyman, Ernie Lepore, and Greg McCulloch. All the papers at the conference are published here, in the order of presentation at the conference. The volume has also been further enhanced by a contribution from Mark Sainsbury. I'm grateful to all the contributors for allowing me to publish their papers in this volume, and to all the participants at the conference for making it such an enjoyable and thought-provoking event.

The papers in this volume all deal, in various respects, with the question of what constraints apply to a proper theory of meaning – either a theory which deals with a part of our language, or a theory for language as a whole, or a theory dealing directly with thought. The contributions by McCulloch and Crane fall into this last category, both exploring the requirements for meaningful mental representations. McCulloch argues against the truth of the claim that one might, possibly, be a brain-in-a-vat. For, he contends, were such a scenario to be in place, the prerequisites for genuine (i.e. meaningful) mental representations would not be met. So, for McCulloch it is our connections to real world objects which are necessary to underpin contentful mental states. The question which interests Crane, however, runs in the other direction, for he considers what we are committed to when we make claims about the existence of the objects of thought. In 'Intentional Objects', he reassesses the status of the kind of intentional objects first proffered by Brentano, and promoted in the contemporary context by Searle. The question posed by Crane is: what is the ontological status of these *prima facie* peculiar objects, and just what is involved in calling them 'objects' in the first place? For if, by labelling them in this way, we mean to claim all intentional objects exist, then it is impossible, contrary to first impressions, to think about non-existent things. His response to this worry is to deny that we mean by 'object' here something like 'entity' or 'thing'; intentional objects are simply the objects of thought, where this does not commit us to any strong claims about their 'real' existence. So while McCulloch argues that the existence of real world objects is a prerequisite for mental content, Crane argues against a potentially parallel move, suggesting that the existence of an object of thought is not sufficient for making any predictions about the constituents of the world.

The other papers in this volume approach the constraints on meaning from the perspective of natural language. Hyman's paper discusses the logical and semantic status of nominalized sentences such as 'the death of Socrates'. The initial question he addresses is whether, as surface form seems to indicate, such nominalizations should be treated as relational descriptions. The answer Hyman proposes here is negative: though such sentences have the structural complexity of a definite description, they have the semantic directness of a name. This negative answer is then shown to have serious repercussions for a range of philosophical issues. For certain well-known accounts (such as Davidson's analysis of action sentences, Grice's account of perception, or Lewis's analysis of belief reports) requires that the nominalized sentences in question (e.g. 'Brutus's killing of Caesar' or 'my perception of a table in front of me') are treated as essentially relational expressions. Yet, if the findings of the first half of Hyman's paper are correct, then such sentences *cannot* be relational descriptions, and thus the proposed analyses (of action, perception and belief) must be rejected.

Finally, then, the papers of Fodor and Lepore, Horwich and Sainsbury explore the question of the theoretical constraints on an adequate theory of meaning for language as a whole. These papers debate the role of compositionality – the idea, roughly, that the meaning of a complex linguistic item is exhausted by the meaning of its constituents and their mode of combination. Fodor and Lepore see the constraint of compositionality as so hard to satisfy that it greatly (perhaps uniquely) limits our choice of acceptable semantic theory. For them, it is a formal, truth-conditional approach to meaning which, alone in this context, is able to satisfy the compositionality constraint. Horwich, on the other hand, sees compositionality as hardly any constraint on theories of meaning at all. Instead, he offers us a 'deflationary' take on the notion (in keeping with his general deflationary stance on meaning), whereby one can state the requirement for compositionality without thereby giving rise to any kind of prejudice about the types of things which can serve as the meanings of lexical primitives.

One way to see their debate emerges in their different stances over what Fodor and Lepore call the 'uniformity thesis' or 'uniformity principle', p. 73 (and which Horwich labels the 'Uniformity Assumption', p. 87). This principle holds that: 'if the meanings of primitives are stereotypes (or uses, or prototypes, or inferential roles, or whatever), then the meanings of the complexes are *also* stereotypes (uses, prototypes, inferential roles, etc.), p. 73. Fodor and Lepore see the uniformity principle as holding in general for natural language. To support this claim they introduce, in the later stages of their paper, a new twist on the usual compositionality considerations. For they question not only whether an account like Horwich's can show that the meaning of a complex linguistic item is exhausted by the meaning of its parts and their mode of combination (compositionality). They also question whether his account can show that the meanings of primitive lexical items depend on the meanings of the complex items in which they appear (e.g. that the meaning of 'dog' supervenes on the meaning of 'dogs bark'). They call this constraint 'reverse compositionality' and suggest that it, together with compositionality per se, shows the uniformity principle to hold good. Horwich, however, rejects the uniformity assumption as unwarranted – it is perfectly possible, he suggests, that the meanings of words are constituted by, say, their use properties, though the meanings of complex linguistic expressions are constituted in some quite other way.

Stepping in to this debate, Sainsbury, in the final paper of the volume, seeks to challenge a common assumption between Fodor and Lepore, and Horwich – namely that compositionality holds for language in general. Sainsbury surveys a range of cases (such as adjectival modification, genitives, and what he calls 'the Travis effect', emerging from the kinds of examples made famous by Charles Travis), which *prima facie*, are problematic for this assumption. For in each case, it appears that the compound expression is ambiguous, even though its parts and their manner of combination are non-ambiguous. If this is correct, then the meaning of the whole must go beyond the meaning of the parts and their mode of composition, and thus each of these cases serves as a putative counterexample to compositionality. The general moral Sainsbury draws from this finding is that specifying the constraints proper to the construction of an adequate theory of meaning will require close and careful consideration of the whole canon of natural language use. We cannot simply assume that a constraint like compositionality holds across the board.

I'd like to close by noting one other theme which unites and divides the following papers (a theme which should not be surprising given the title of the volume). This is the issue of the relationship between meaning and representation. For the question which these essays return to again and again is: how do formal representations (either purely syntactically described, or representations within some logical system) map to semantic representations? It is an idea which has been commonplace in the philosophy of mind and language from at least Wittgenstein's *Tractatus Logico-Philosophicus* that specifications of logical form will ultimately be informative as to the meaning properties of expressions. Indeed, this idea forms an integral part of the kind of formal semantic theory advocated by Fodor and Lepore, where the input to the theory of meaning just is formally described representations of natural language expressions.

However, at least two of the papers here express a deep scepticism about this fundamental assumption. For instance, Horwich sees it as one of the great attractions of abandoning the truth-conditional approach to meaning that it frees us from the 'commitment to cram every natural language construction into the narrow mould of predicate logic' (p. 81); while Hyman's paper suggests that there may be substantial differences between the semantic structure of sentences in natural language and their usual paraphrases in logical notation. Meanwhile, McCulloch forces us to question what is required for a formally described object to count as a meaningful representation at all; on his account, a brain-in-a-vat might get the syntax of representation, as it were, whilst lacking all of the semantics. Amongst other issues, then, it is the deep differences on the question of how formally described objects connect to the semantic realm which these papers admirably help to circumscribe and illuminate.

Emma Borg
Associate Editor, Ratio
Department of Philosophy
The University of Reading
e.g.n.borg@rdg.ac.uk

CHAPTER 2

–INGS AND –ERS

John Hyman

Abstract
This paper is about the semantic structure of verbal and deverbal noun phrases. The focus is on noun phrases which describe actions, perceptions, sensations and beliefs. It is commonly thought that actions are movements of parts of the agent's body which we typically describe in terms of their effects, and that perceptions are slices of sensible experience which we typically describe in terms of their causes. And many philosophers hold that sensations and beliefs are states of the central nervous system which we generally describe in terms of their typical causes and effects. For example 'Brutus's killing of Caesar' is thought to describe a movement of a part of Brutus's body – e.g. the thrust of an arm – in terms of one of its effects, namely, Caesar's death. And 'Hyman's visual perception of a table in front of him' is thought to describe the visual experience I'm having right now in terms of its cause. The object of the paper is to show that these doctrines misrepresent the semantic structure of verbal and deverbal noun phrases.

1

I shall begin with a quotation from a paper by Wilfrid Sellars. In the passage that I want to quote, Sellars makes a comment about the sentences 'Jones has an impression' (he means some kind of visual impression) and 'Jones wore a smile'. This is what he says:

> Another way of putting this is to draw a distinction between *real* relations, such as 'to the left of', and *nominal* relations, such as 'has' or 'wore'. The 'nominal' character of the latter would be bound up with their eliminability in accordance with the schema 'x is R_n to a $N_v \leftrightarrow$ x V' where 'R_n' stands for the nominal relation, and 'N_v' for the verbal noun corresponding to the verb 'V'.[1]

---

[1] Sellars 1967, p. 287.

Sellars is saying that the main verb in a sentence like 'Jones wore a smile' doesn't really express a relation. 'Jones wore a smile' may look like the sentence 'Jones wore a hat', but the appearance is deceptive. And this is connected with the fact that the 'nominal' relation expressed by the verb 'wore' in 'Jones wore a smile' can be eliminated, by paraphrasing the sentence as 'Jones smiled'.

As I shall explain shortly, I believe that Sellars is right about this. And I believe this has some important implications in the theory of action and perception, and in the philosophy of mind, which I shall spell out in due course. But first, I want to make some general comments about definite descriptions and about verbal and deverbal noun-phrases.

2

A definite description is sometimes defined as a term which consists of the definite article followed by a noun-phrase: e.g., 'the author of Waverley', 'the death of Socrates', 'the cube root of eight'. But this definition is unsatisfactory, for two reasons.

The first reason is that it excludes terms like 'Lewis's cat', 'Waverley's author' and 'Socrates' death', which don't begin with the definite article, but which mean the same as terms that do. And of course there are languages that have no articles – Latin and Polish, for example. But 'The author of Waverley was Scotch' has an exact translation in Latin or Polish, and the controversy about definite descriptions is just as much about the interpretation of these sentences as it is about their English counterparts.

The second reason is that part of the point of introducing the idea of a definite description is to contrast it with the idea of a proper name. But there are many proper names that consist of the definite article followed by a noun-phrase. For example, 'The King's Arms' is the name of a pub in Oxford, and 'The Origin of Species' is the name of a book. Neither of these names could be described as a 'meaningless mark', which is how Mill sometimes describes a proper name. All the same, they are proper names and not descriptions.[2]

---

[2] Far from being meaningless, names quite often convey information about their bearers. For example, 'Kristin Lavransdatter' is the name of a woman whose father was called Lavran, 'Discours de la méthode de bien conduire sa raison, et chercher la vérité dans les sciences' is the name of a book, and 'I can't believe it's not butter!' is the name of a margarine.

I do not intend to define the term 'definite description'. But I shall use it broadly enough to include any term which means the same as one which consists of the definite article followed by a noun-phrase, and whose meaning we need to be aware of, in order to understand a sentence in which it occurs. This includes the cases where we use the genitive case instead of the definite article and it excludes proper names.

It also includes 'the glasses' in the sentence 'The glasses are in the cupboard' and 'the butter' in the sentence 'The butter is rancid', despite the fact that these sentences cannot be paraphrased in the way that Russell paraphrases 'The author of Waverley was Scotch'. For some purposes, it would be useful to demarcate a smaller class of expressions. But for my purposes this will do fine.

3

There are three further points I want to make about definite descriptions and proper names. First, definite descriptions describe things belonging to various categories – including people ('the author of Waverley'), places ('the capital of Finland'), events ('the death of Socrates'), and periods of time ('the day after Christmas').

Second, there are expressions that fall in between proper names and definite descriptions, such as 'the Prophet Isaiah' and 'the City of Rome'. It is probably best to construe this sort of expression as a combination of a name and a *determinative*, i.e. an expression that indicates the kind of thing to which the bearer of the name belongs. When the word 'of' links the two, it is simply an appositive device, like the genitive of apposition in 'Dublin's fair city'. In fact the Latin for 'the City of Rome' is 'Urbs Roma', which is in the nominative case, and not 'Urbs Romae'.

The third point – which is the most important for my purposes – is that some definite descriptions are *relational* descriptions. By a relation, I mean a way in which one thing can stand to another thing, or several things can stand to one another.[3] For example,

[3] Prior 1976, p. 29, remarks that the general notion of a many-termed relation seems to be a relatively recent one, and suggests that it was formed by about 1870.

It is debatable whether acts are relations. (See Kenny 1963, ch. 7.) Certainly, an act is not a way in which one thing can stand to another thing. For acts are dynamic, and not static. But the argument in this paper does not turn on the distinction between acts and relations, and for the most part I shall ignore it in what follows.

there are relations of comparison, such as being hotter than or wiser than; spatial and temporal relations, such as being inside, west of or earlier than; cognitive relations, such as being a witness of or being acquainted with; and relations that result from actions, such as being the father of, the author of or the owner of. By a relational description, I do not mean a description of a relation. I mean a description that describes a thing in terms of a relation. For example, 'the author of Waverley' describes a man by mentioning a book he wrote. As P.F. Strawson puts it, it catches its man in a relation, and the relation is *being the author of*, or simply *authorship*. Again, 'Lewis's cat' describes a cat by mentioning its owner. So in this case the relation is *being the owner of*, or simply *ownership*. (Cats like to think of it as *co-habitation*; but we know better.)[4]

4

So much for definite descriptions in general. Now 'the death of Socrates' and 'the fall of Constantinople' are evidently definite descriptions. But they are definite descriptions of a particular sort, which I shall call *nominalizations of sentences*.

We can form a nominalization of a sentence by a simple procedure. We simply replace the main verb of the sentence with the corresponding verbal or deverbal noun and then either we put the subject of the sentence into the genitive case or we combine the noun with the definite article and insert prepositions where they are required, to link the resulting noun-phrase with the subject and object of the verb. In this way, 'Socrates died' yields 'Socrates' death' or 'The death of Socrates', 'Constantinople fell' yields 'Constantinople's fall' or 'The fall of Constantinople', 'Brutus killed Caesar' yields 'Brutus's killing of Caesar' or 'The killing of Caesar by Brutus', and so on.

The rules that govern the construction of these expressions are not very complicated. But it would be a digression to explain them here. The question I want to address is the following one:

---

⁴ Notice that if Smith himself is the man who shaves Smith, 'the man who shaves Smith' is a relational description of Smith. But although Brown may be the same man as Smith, 'the same man as Smith' cannot be a relational description of Brown, because one man cannot be the same man as another, and hence *being the same man as* is not, in the sense in which I am using the term, a relation. I regard 'the same man as Smith' as an elaboration (as opposed to an abbreviation) of 'the man Smith', which is comparable to 'the Prophet Isaiah' and 'the City of Rome', and hence not strictly speaking a definite description at all.

are these terms, or are some of them, relational descriptions? Do they sometimes catch the things we use them to describe in a relation? I shall begin with 'the death of Socrates'.

5

Suppose 'the death of Socrates' *is* a relational description. Suppose it picks out an event – a death – in terms of a relation between this event and Socrates. What *is* the relation? The answer that occurs to many people first is: *undergoing* or *being the subject of*. But arguably we don't undergo our own deaths, unless we survive them. So it is probably wise to stick with *being the subject of*. Interestingly, though, Donald Davidson answers the question differently. He says that the relation is *dying*. In fact his example in the sentence I shall quote is flying, not dying. What he says is this:

> Flying is basically a relation between an event of flying and a thing that flies.[5]

Davidson makes it clear that he is using the verb 'fly' intransitively. Hence, if what he says is true, dying is basically a relation between an event of dying and a thing that dies.

It sounds a little odd to say that dying is a relation, because the verb 'died', in the sentence 'Socrates died', doesn't look as if it expresses a relation. Intransitive verbs don't. But appear-

---

[5] Davidson 1985, p. 232. It should be noted that some remarks by Davidson (which were, however, made some fifteen years earlier) suggest that he may have intended a rather special interpretation of this claim. He writes as follows: 'all I *mean* by saying that ['Spirit of St. Louis flew'] has the logical form of an existentially quantified sentence, and that ['flew'] is a [two-]place predicate is that a theory of truth meeting Tarski's criteria would entail that this sentence is true if and only if there exists . . . etc.' (Davidson 1980a, p. 143. I have replaced Davidson's own example.) If we bear this remark in mind, and if we also make the assumption that all Davidson means by claiming that flying is basically a relation is that 'flew' is a two-place predicate, the claim amounts to this: a theory of truth for English meeting Tarski's criteria would entail the theorem: 'Spirit of St. Louis flew' is true if and only if $((x)$ (Flew (Spirit of St. Louis, x)). It is no part of my purpose in this paper to dispute this claim.

Nor do I wish to deny that the only logical paraphrases of the sentences 'Spirit of St. Louis flew gracefully' and 'Spirit of St. Louis flew' which will ensure that the inference we make by dropping the adverb corresponds to a correct sequent of the predicate calculus will use a predicate with an extra place to represent the verb. As it happens, Davidson's logical paraphrases can be improved on. For if we follow Davidson, the inference from 'Brutus killed Caesar' to 'Caesar died' does not correspond to a correct sequent; and there is a different method of paraphrase with which it does. (See Alvarez 1999, p. 225.) But the argument in this paper does not, in my view, provide any additional ammunition for someone unhappy with Davidson's formalizations.

ances can be deceptive. For example, the sentence 'Socrates ate' is grammatically impeccable. But it has often been said – rightly or wrongly – that the verb 'ate' does express a relation here, and that we can paraphrase 'Socrates ate' as 'Socrates ate something', if we want to make this explicit.

If Davidson is right, the sentence 'Socrates died' is similar. The verb 'died' expresses a relation between Socrates and an event; and we can make this explicit by paraphrasing 'Socrates died' as 'Socrates died something'. In this case, the something is an event. But the pronoun 'something' commonly ranges over events. 'Something happened', we say. In fact it's the title of a novel.

So, if 'the death of Socrates' *is* a relational description, which relation is it to be, *being the subject of* or *dying?* The answer is that we don't need to choose. Because either way, if we claim that 'the death of Socrates' is a relational description, we imply that the verb 'died' in the sentence 'Socrates died' expresses a relation. If we choose *being the subject of*, the paraphrase of 'Socrates died' which makes this explicit packs more information into the noun: 'Socrates was the subject of a death'. If we choose *dying*, the paraphrase packs more information into the verb: 'Socrates died something'. But either way, we can decide whether 'the death of Socrates' is a relational description by deciding whether the verb 'died' in the sentence 'Socrates died' expresses a relation.

6

As I have said, it does not look as if it does. But it is easy enough to produce a paraphrase of 'Socrates died' in which the main verb does look as if it expresses a relation, even if we are reluctant to tolerate the artificiality, or grammatical oddity, of the paraphrases I mentioned a moment ago, because 'Socrates died' can be paraphrased as 'Socrates met his death'. Hence, we can decide whether 'the death of Socrates' is a relational description by deciding whether the verb 'died' expresses a relation in the sentence 'Socrates died', despite not appearing to; or whether, on the contrary, the verb 'met' doesn't express a relation in the sentence 'Socrates met his death', although it looks as if it does.

In fact 'Socrates met his death' is an example of a fairly common construction in English. One can take a bath and have a chat. One can make a choice or a promise. And so on. Often the main verb in this kind of sentence will be one of a limited number of common verbs, such as 'have', 'do', 'give', 'make' or 'take'. But it is sometimes cognate with the noun-phrase. For example, if Socrates lived well and died peacefully, then he lived a good life and died a peaceful death. Sentences like 'Socrates took a bath' are said to have eventive objects; and sentences like 'Socrates died a peaceful death' are said to have cognate objects.

Now as we saw at the beginning, Sellars claims that the verb 'wore' in the sentence 'Jones wore a smile' doesn't really express a relation; and he says that this is bound up with its eliminability. In other words, it is bound up with the fact that 'Jones wore a smile' can be paraphrased as 'Jones smiled'. And of course if Sellars is right, the same applies to 'Socrates died a peaceful death', which can be paraphrased as 'Socrates died peacefully', and to 'Socrates had a chat, took a bath and met his death', which can be paraphrased as 'Socrates chatted, bathed and died'.

I think Sellars *is* right about this, but eliminability by paraphrase isn't by itself a convincing reason, because if one sentence is a paraphrase of another sentence, the second sentence is a paraphrase of the first. In other words, the relation *being a paraphrase of* is a symmetric relation. And Sellars does not provide a reason for holding that the verbs in 'Jones wore a smile' and 'Socrates met his death' don't really express relations, in spite of the superficial grammar of these sentences; instead of holding that the verbs in 'Jones smiled' and 'Socrates died' do really express relations, in spite of the superficial grammar of *these* sentences.

But there is a reason. In fact there are several, and I shall mention two. In the first place, if the main verb of a sentence with a cognate object expressed a relation, then as C.J.F. Williams shows, some evidently fallacious arguments would be valid. For example, 'Bonzo fights only what he hates; Bonzo fights many cats; *ergo* Bonzo hates many cats' is a valid argument; but 'Bonzo fights only what he hates; Bonzo fights many fights; *ergo* Bonzo hates many fights' is not.[6]

Secondly, a nominalization of a sentence in which the main verb expresses a relation is not a description of one of the relata. For example, take the sentence 'Rachel is the sister of Leah'. 'The x such that x is the sister of Leah' and 'the x such that Rachel is the sister of x' are definite descriptions of the two sisters; but 'Rachel's being a sister of Leah' is not a description of either of them. Again, take the sentence 'Judas kissed Jesus'.

---

6 Williams 1989, p. 144.

'The x such that Judas kissed x' and 'the x such that x kissed Jesus' are descriptions of the parties to a kiss. But 'Judas's kissing of Jesus' is a description of a kiss*ing*, i.e. a kiss. And the kiss*ing* is neither the kiss*er* nor the kissed. But the nominalization of 'Socrates met his death' *is* a description of what Socrates met, when he met his death. Because of course when Socrates met his death, their meeting *was* his death. Hence Sellars was right. The main verb in the sentence 'Socrates met his death' does not express a relation. And so the paraphrase 'Socrates met his death' disguises the semantic structure of the sentence 'Socrates died', and not vice versa. It does not follow that there is no relation in which Socrates stood to his death. And in fact there is evidently at least one such relation, because Socrates committed suicide, and a man who commits suicide causes his own death. But it does follow that the verb 'died' in the sentence 'Socrates died' does not express a relation; and hence that 'the death of Socrates' is not a relational description.

7

What about a description that is derived from a sentence in which the main verb is transitive? For example 'Brutus's killing of Caesar' is a nominalization of the sentence 'Brutus killed Caesar'. Is 'Brutus's killing of Caesar' a relational description?

It is certainly possible to derive relational descriptions from the sentence 'Brutus killed Caesar', namely, 'the x such that x killed Caesar' and 'the x such that Brutus killed x'. But – assuming that Brutus alone killed Caesar, and that Caesar was his only victim – these describe Brutus and Caesar respectively. Whereas of course 'Brutus's killing of Caesar' mentions both of them, but describes an act. So what should we say about 'Brutus's killing of Caesar'?

The argument is exactly parallel to the argument about 'the death of Socrates'. 'The death of Socrates' cannot be a relational description unless the verb 'died' in the sentence 'Socrates died' expresses a two-place relation; and by parity of reasoning 'Brutus's killing of Caesar' cannot be a relational description unless the verb 'killed' in the sentence 'Brutus killed Caesar' expresses a *three*-place relation. In other words, if dying is basically a relation between an event of dying and something that dies, then killing is basically a relation between an act of killing, something that kills and a victim.

As with 'Socrates died', we can devise a (clumsy) paraphrase in which the main verb is nominalized and another verb which appears to express a relation is introduced, viz. 'Brutus performed the killing of Caesar'. (Paraphrasing 'A murdered B' as 'A committed the murder of B' is also clumsy, but less so.) But the result of this operation is another sentence with an eventive object; the performance of the killing and the killing performed are one and the same act; and hence the verb 'performed' does not express a relation.

8

I think it should be obvious by now that a nominalization of a sentence is never a relational description. Whether the main verb of the original sentence is transitive or intransitive, the verbal noun-phrase cannot catch the act or event or state of affairs reported by the sentence in a relation. In a sense, a relational description takes an indirect route to its destination, and reaches it via something else. For example, 'the author of Waverley' reaches Scott via Waverley, and the route from Waverley to Scott is authorship. But the route from 'Waverley' to Waverley is a direct one. If the argument so far is correct, a nominalization of a sentence has the semantic complexity of a definite description, but the directness of a name.

But why does this matter? It matters because it has become common among philosophers to make claims that imply that various nominalizations of sentences *are* relational descriptions. Here are some examples: first, nominalizations of sentences reporting acts, such as 'Brutus's killing of Caesar'; secondly, nominalizations of sentences reporting perceptions, such as 'my perception of a table in front of me'; thirdly, nominalizations of sentences reporting sensations and beliefs, such as 'Jack's headache' and 'Joe's believing that lemurs are carnivorous'. Nominalizations of sentences reporting acts are held to describe either movements of the agent's body or events inside the agent's body in terms of their effects – for example by Davidson and Hornsby. Nominalizations of sentences reporting perceptions are held to describe impressions or experiences in terms of their causes – for example by Grice and Strawson. And nominalizations of sentences reporting sensations and beliefs are held to describe events in or states of the nervous system in terms of their typical causes *and* effects – for example by Armstrong and Lewis.

9

I shall comment on all of these cases, beginning with action and perception. In Davidson's article, 'Agency', he invites us to imagine that a queen killed a king by pouring poison into his ear, and that she poured the poison by holding the vial by his ear and moving her hand, or rotating her wrist. In this case, Davidson argues, 'the killing . . . did not differ from the movement of the hand'.[7] He says that these acts are not 'numerically distinct'.[8]

If Davidson is right, the queen's killing of the king *was* a movement of her hand; this movement was a killing because it was an act that caused a death; and if we describe it as a killing, we are describing it in terms of a relation – the causal relation between the act itself and its effect. This is how Davidson puts it: 'the description of an event is made to include reference to a consequence'.[9] And when he returns to this theme in a later essay, he says the noun-phrases 'my poisoning of the victim', 'my killing of the victim' and 'my murdering of the victim' are expressions which 'describe actions . . . in terms of their causal relations'.[10]

Now for perception. Strawson states the doctrine I want to comment on as follows:

> It is a necessary condition of an M-experience being the M-perception it seems to be that the experience should be causally dependent on corresponding M-facts.[11]

This statement of the doctrine involves some technical terminology, but the terminology can be explained quite simply. First, an *M-experience* is the experience one is having if it sensibly seems to one as if one is perceiving an object or an array of objects. For example, right now it sensibly seems to me as if I am seeing a table in front of me. Secondly, an *M-perception* is an instance of someone's actually perceiving something. For example, right now I actually am seeing a table in front of me. And thirdly, an *M-fact* is the fact that an object or an array of objects exists. For example, right now there *is* a table in front of me.

If Strawson is right, the M-experience I am having right now qualifies as a perception of a table in front of me, and I can

[7] Davidson 1980a, p. 58.
[8] Ibid., p. 56.
[9] Ibid., p. 58.
[10] Davidson 1980b, p. 178.
[11] Strawson 1974, p. 73.

describe it as a perception of a table in front of me, only because it is causally dependent on the fact that there *is* a table in front of me. Hence, once again, the noun-phrase 'my perception of a table in front of me' is a relational description of the visual experience I am having now. It describes this experience by mentioning an object that was involved in causing it.

So we have two ideas. First, we have the idea that acts are changes in the agent's body – movements of his limbs, perhaps – which we typically describe in terms of their effects. For example, 'Brutus's killing of Caesar' describes a movement of a part of Brutus's body – the thrust of an arm, perhaps – in terms of Caesar's death. And secondly, the idea that perceptions are 'slices of sensible experience' – the phrase is Strawson's[12] – which occur in our minds because of the influence of the environment on our sense organs, and which we typically describe in terms of their causes.[13]

These two ideas stem from a long and powerful tradition in philosophical thinking, which encourages us to shrink our acts and experiences so that they fit within our skin. We imagine that the act itself is a change in the body's shape, or its position. Whatever else we mention is extraneous. And we imagine that a perception is an episode inside the skull, or in the soul. But Brutus's killing of Caesar cannot be a movement of Brutus's arm, because if it were, 'Brutus's killing of Caesar' would be a relational description of it: it would describe the movement in terms of its relation to a death. And my perception of a table in front of me cannot be an episode inside my skull or a purely spiritual occurrence, because if it were, 'my perception of a table in front of me' would describe this episode in terms of its relation to a table. Hence, the semantic structure of these descriptions disproves the imaginary conception we have inherited of the things that they describe.

But if acts are not movements of the agent's body, which we typically describe in terms of their effects, and if perceptions are not 'slices of sensible experience', which occur in the minds of

---

[12] Strawson 1979, p. 43.

[13] The analogy between these ideas is noted by Jennifer Hornsby, who writes as follows: 'If I am right about action, and if those who have recently advocated causal theories of perception are right about perception, then there is an obvious analogy between the concepts. To describe an event as a perception (a perceiving of something) is to describe it in terms of its causes: to describe an event as an action is to describe it in terms of its effects.' Hornsby 1980, p. 111.

sentient animals, and which we typically describe in terms of their causes, what are acts and perceptions?

One plausible answer is that acts and perceptions are not things that we typically describe in terms of relations: they are themselves relations, or better, instances of relations. Thus a perception is an instance of a cognitive relation, obtaining between a sentient animal and a perceptible object; and an act is an instance of causation, obtaining between an agent and an event. For example, Brutus's killing of Caesar was Brutus's causing of Caesar's death. And Brutus's extending of his arm was Brutus's causing of this extension. Hence both of these acts are causings; and causings are instances of the relation expressed by the verb 'cause'.[14]

10

Next I want to say something in turn about sensations and about beliefs. One of the examples I gave earlier of a relational description was 'Lewis's cat'. I picked this phrase in honour of David Lewis, and with a particular passage from an article by Lewis in mind. The article is 'Mad Pain and Martian Pain', and Lewis states the doctrine that he wants to defend in it as follows. 'The concept of pain,' he writes, 'or indeed of any other experience or mental state, is the concept of a state that occupies a certain causal role, a state with certain typical causes and effects.' He continues as follows:

> If pain is identical to a certain neural state, the identity is contingent. Whether it holds is one of the things that varies from one possible world to another. But take care. I do not say that here we have two states, pain and some neural state, that are contingently identical, identical at this world but different at another. Since I'm serious about the identity, we have not two states but one. This one state, this neural state which is pain, is not contingently identical to itself. It does not differ from itself at any world. Nothing does. What's true is, rather, that the concept and the name of pain contingently apply to some neural state at this world, but do not apply to it at another. Similarly, it is a contingent truth that Bruce is our cat, but it's wrong to say that Bruce and our cat are contingently

identical. Our cat Bruce is necessarily self-identical. What is contingent is that the nonrigid concept of being our cat applies to Bruce rather than to some other cat, or none.[15]

According to Lewis pain is a neural state. But if I call this neural state 'pain', I describe it in terms of its typical causes and effects. For example, if a headache is keeping me awake, it is a neural state that is keeping me awake, whether I realize this or not. And if I *say* that a headache is keeping me awake, I pick out this neural state by implicitly adverting to the kinds of events by which it is typically caused, and the kinds of events that it typically causes.

But take care. 'The kinds of events by which it is typically caused' does not mean the kinds of events by which a particular *instance* of the state is typically caused. An instance of the state has, no doubt, its causes and effects; but it has no *typical* causes and effects. It cannot be caused by one kind of thing in typical cases, and by another kind of thing in atypical cases, because an instance has no cases. It does not recur. 'The kinds of events by which it is typically caused' means the kinds of events by which typical instances of this state are caused, and 'the kinds of events which it typically causes' means the kinds of events which typical instances of this state cause.

Lewis holds that whatever state pain is, it could have been a different state. If neural state X is the state that occupies the causal role we associate with pain, then pain *is* neural state X. But it could have been state Y. Because state Y could have occupied this causal role instead, if (as Lewis puts it) 'the relevant causal relations had been different'. Hence, he also holds that if I use the word 'pain', it is a contingent fact that the name I use applies to the state it does apply to. It is a contingent fact that 'pain' applies to neural state X, in the same way as it is a contingent fact that 'Lewis's cat' applies to Bruce.

But if the concepts of pain and headache are the concepts of states with certain typical causes and effects, it also follows that 'the pain in Jack's knee' and 'Jack's headache' are *relational* descriptions, since they describe states in terms of their causal relations. As I explained earlier, they take an indirect route to their destination, and reach it via something else. 'Lewis's cat' reaches Bruce via Lewis, and the route from Lewis to Bruce is ownership. And if the concepts of pain and headache are the

[15] Lewis 1980, p. 218.

concepts of states that occupy a certain causal role, then 'the pain in Jack's knee' and 'Jack's headache' also take an indirect route to the states they describe, via the kinds of events which pains in knees and headaches are typically caused by, and the kinds of events which they typically cause.

11

Now consider the sentence 'Jack has a headache'. I hope it is clear that the verb 'has' in this sentence is being used in the same way as the verb 'met' in the sentence 'Socrates met his death', the verb 'wore' in the sentence 'Jones wore a smile' and, closest of all, the verb 'has' in the sentence 'Jack has a nosebleed'. The verb 'has' in these two sentences – 'Jack has a headache' and 'Jack has a nosebleed' – is not being used to express a relation. It is simply a common verb – like 'take' and 'make' – combined with an eventive object.

It is sometimes said that sensations are not *objects* that we experience, but kinds *of* experience; or that sensations are not *things* we can be aware of, but *states* we can be in. But if we say one of these things, we run the risk of seeming to deny what is obviously true, namely, that we can experience or be aware of sensations. And we impose a restriction on the use of the words 'object' and 'thing' which a special tone of voice or the use of italics is sometimes expected to convey, but cannot possibly explain. However, we can steer clear of these unsatisfactory claims without missing the important point that having a headache is not a matter of standing in a relation to something, and *a fortiori* that it is not a matter of standing in a cognitive relation to something.

So, like 'Socrates met his death' and 'Jones wore a smile', the sentences 'Jack has a headache' and 'Jack has a nosebleed' combine a common verb with an eventive object. And just as 'Socrates met his death' can be paraphrased as 'Socrates died' and 'Jones wore a smile' can be paraphrased as 'Jones smiled', 'Jack has a headache' can be paraphrased as 'Jack's head aches' and 'Jack has a nosebleed' can be paraphrased as 'Jack's nose bleeds'. (I shall ignore the difference between the habitual 'bleeds' and the progressive 'is bleeding'.)

But now it should be obvious that 'Jack's headache' and 'Jack's nosebleed' cannot be relational descriptions. Because they are both nominalizations of sentences, and a nominalization of a sentence cannot be a relational description. 'Jack's headache' – which means the same as 'the aching of Jack's head' – is a nominalization of the sentence 'Jack's head aches'; and 'Jack's nosebleed' – which means the same as 'the bleeding of Jack's nose' – is a nominalization of the sentence 'Jack's nose bleeds'. Hence, 'Jack's headache' and 'Jack's nosebleed' cannot catch the things they describe in a relation, any more than 'Socrates' death' and 'Jones's smile' can. But if 'Jack's headache' isn't a relational description, it cannot pick out a state in terms of its typical causes and effects. Hence, the concept of headache cannot be the concept of a state that occupies a certain causal role.

The idea that the terms in which we typically describe sensations only apply to them contingently has been debated extensively. Saul Kripke (among others) has argued that this idea is false. Whereas David Lewis (among others) has argued for the opposite view. But the question of whether these noun-phrases are relational descriptions has been neglected. Perhaps this is because philosophers are reluctant to acknowledge that grammar has a bearing on philosophy. Everyone agrees that we should be open-minded about the sorts of propositions that can prove or disprove philosophical doctrines. No one wants to argue against being open-minded. For example, if a philosopher attempted to prove the existence of God from the premise that some things move, or from the premise that ginger is hot, no one would object that kinematics cannot have a bearing on theology, or that God's existence cannot be deduced from a fact about root vegetables. But grammar is not a popular source of knowledge among philosophers these days.

As it turns out, the fact that 'Jack's headache' is a nominalization of a sentence does not tell us *much* about sensations. It does not even tell us enough to distinguish between headaches and nosebleeds, and as we know, these are very different things. But it tells us enough to know that the concept of headache is not the concept of a functional state, for example, one that will turn out to be a state of the nervous system. For that matter, the fact that 'Jack's nosebleed' is a nominalization of a sentence does not tell us much about nosebleeds either. But it does entail that the concept of a nosebleed is not the concept of a functional state of the venous system.

12

When we turn to beliefs, one preliminary point needs to be borne in mind. The term 'belief' – like the terms 'statement', 'announcement', 'assertion', 'claim', etc. – can be used in two distinct but connected ways. It can be used to mean *either* something that is believed *or* an instance of someone's believing something. And, as has often been noted, these are quite different things. Something believed is, in one familiar use of this term, a *proposition* – an item in a creed, so to speak. Whereas someone's believing something is an instance of a state of mind – the credence rather than the creed.

Suppose, for example, that Joe believes lemurs are carnivorous. If Joe's belief is true or false, denied by Jim, or consistent with some evidence, it is *what Joe believes* – namely, that lemurs are carnivorous – that is true or false, denied by Jim, or consistent with some evidence. An instance of a state of mind is not the sort of thing that *can* be true or false, etc. If it were, it would also be the sort of thing that can be entailed by Euclid's axioms. But if Joe's belief is silly or unreasonable, it is *Joe's believing that lemurs are carnivorous* that is silly or unreasonable. In other words, it is silly or unreasonable of Joe to believe this. It cannot be silly or unreasonable that lemurs are carnivorous. Whose silliness or unreasonableness would it be?

Now if it is claimed that the description 'Joe's belief that lemurs are carnivorous' applies to whatever state occupies a certain causal role, 'Joe's belief that lemurs are carnivorous' must be taken to mean Joe's believing that lemurs are carnivorous, and not what Joe believes. Because what Joe believes is evidently not a state. But 'Joe's believing that lemurs are carnivorous' is a nominalization of the sentence 'Joe believes that lemurs are carnivorous'. Hence it cannot be a relational description, and it cannot pick out a state in terms of its typical causes and effects. Hence the claim that 'Joe's belief that lemurs are carnivorous' applies to whatever state occupies a certain causal role is false.

13

Finally, I want to consider an objection, which is directed in particular towards my remarks about descriptions of acts. I said earlier that if Brutus alone killed Caesar, the relational description 'the x such that x killed Caesar' describes Brutus. But to kill a man is to cause his death. Hence, if Brutus alone killed Caesar, 'the x such that x caused Caesar's death' must also describe Brutus. But Davidson denies that this is strictly true. He writes as follows:

although we say that the agent caused the death of the victim, that is, that he killed him, this is an elliptical way of saying that some act of the agent . . . caused the death of the victim.[16] If this is correct, 'Brutus's killing of Caesar' must also be an ellipsis, and it may appear that restoring the missing phrase will reveal a relational description, such as 'the act of Brutus's which caused Caesar's death', which evidently does describe an act in terms of one of its effects. So we need to consider two questions. First, is 'Brutus killed Caesar' an ellipsis? And secondly, if it is, does it follow that 'Brutus's killing of Caesar' is, after all, a relational description?

It is not difficult to see why philosophers invoke ellipses. A hidden piece of meaning can preserve a semantic theory in much the same way as a hidden heavenly body can save an astronomical one. But in this case there are several reasons for thinking that Davidson is mistaken. In the first place, 'Brutus killed Caesar' is not grammatically incomplete as it stands, unlike, say, 'Peter is tired but James is not [tired]', 'I'm happy if you are [happy]' and '[It is] lovely to see you'.

Secondly, the supposedly missing expression is neither an exact copy of the antecedent, as it is in the first two standard examples mentioned above, nor even precisely recoverable, as it is in all three. Is the complete sentence supposed to be '*Some act of* Brutus*'s* killed Caesar' or 'Brutus*'s doing or failing to do something* killed Caesar'? Or are we supposed to delete the word 'killed', producing '*Some act of* Brutus*'s caused* ~~killed~~ Caesar*'s death*', or 'Brutus*'s doing or failing to do something caused* ~~killed~~ Caesar*'s death*'?

Thirdly, if saying that Brutus killed Caesar were an elliptical way of saying that some act of Brutus's caused Caesar's death, it would not be possible to understand the sentence 'Brutus killed Caesar' without knowing that if Brutus killed Caesar, he did so by doing or failing to do something else, just as it is not possible to understand the sentence 'Peter is tired but James is not' without knowing that if Peter is tired but James is not, then James is not tired. But with 'Brutus killed Caesar' this *is* possible. Many people believe that merely wanting someone to die, without doing anything about it, can sometimes cause that person's death. They are certainly mistaken. But it does not follow that they cannot understand the sentence 'Brutus killed Caesar'.

[16] Davidson 1980a, p. 49.

Fourthly, 'Brutus killed Caesar' and 'Some act of Brutus's caused Caesar's death' do not have the same meaning. For if they did have the same meaning, then by parity of reasoning 'Brutus raised his arm' would mean the same as 'Some act of Brutus's caused his arm to rise'. But Brutus *could* raise his arm without doing so by doing or failing to do something else, because raising one's arm, unlike killing someone, is something one can do immediately. (Philosophers who deny this are at liberty to vary the example.) But one sentence cannot be elliptical for another unless they have the same meaning.

The only reply to this argument I am aware of is to claim that the sentence 'Brutus raised his arm' is ambiguous; that what it means depends upon whether or not the speaker has an immediate act in mind; and that in one meaning it is elliptical, but in the other not. But this is unconvincing. It is true that 'Brutus raised his arm' does not tell us whether he did so by doing something else. But 'Brutus raised his glass' does not tell us whether he did so by lifting it with his hand, or with a Heath Robinsonian contraption of some sort. This uncertainty does not imply that 'Brutus raised his glass' is ambiguous, or that in one meaning it is elliptical for 'Some event which was caused by some act of Brutus's caused his glass to rise'; and the corresponding uncertainty does not imply that 'Brutus raised his arm' is ambiguous, or that in one meaning it is elliptical for 'Some act of Brutus's caused his arm to rise'.[17, 18]

For these reasons, I do not accept that 'Brutus killed Caesar' is an ellipsis. But suppose I am mistaken about this. Does it follow that 'Brutus's killing of Caesar' is a relational description, which describes an act in terms of one of its effects? It does not. For if

[17] This point is argued at greater length in Alvarez 1999, pp. 235f. Cf. Parsons 1990, p. 116.

[18] If the sentence 'Some act of Brutus's caused Caesar's death' can be paraphrased as 'Brutus killed Caesar by doing or failing to do something', and if we follow Davidson in using the term 'act' extremely liberally, so that failing to do something can also be an act, then 'Brutus killed Caesar' and 'Some act of Brutus's caused Caesar's death' are logically equivalent. For 'Brutus killed Caesar by doing or failing to do something' entails that Brutus killed Caesar. And Brutus could not possibly have killed Caesar except by doing or failing to do something. God may be able to kill a man immediately – by sheer volition, as it were – but not Brutus.

But logical equivalence does not imply sameness of meaning. There are many examples of logically equivalent sentences which evidently differ in meaning. For example, 'Socrates died' and 'Socrates died if and only if 2+2 = 4' are logically equivalent, but it is clear that they do not have the same meaning, because '2+2 = 4' means something, and so the addition of the phrase 'if and only if 2+2 = 4' cannot leave the meaning of a sentence unaltered. Again, all tautologies are logically equivalent, but 'Either it's raining or it isn't' does not have the same meaning as 'Either he'll arrive on time or he won't'.

'Brutus killed Caesar' is elliptical for 'Some act of Brutus's caused Caesar's death', then the nominalization of the first sentence is elliptical for the nominalization of the second, i.e. 'Brutus's killing of Caesar' is elliptical for 'some act of Brutus's causing Caesar's death'. But whatever this phrase may be thought to describe, it does not describe an act of Brutus's, because it does not describe an act at all. A causing of a death by an agent is an act; but a causing of a death by an act, if there is such a thing, is not. And if it does not describe an act, *a fortiori* it does not describe an act in terms of one of its effects. To suppose that it does is to confuse it with one of the relational descriptions which *can* be derived from the sentence 'Some act of Brutus's caused Caesar's death', namely, 'the act of Brutus's which caused Caesar's death'.

So the objection fails; and it seems that two mistakes conspired to produce it. The first is to detect ellipsis where there is no such thing. The second is to confuse the nominalization 'the killing of Caesar' and the relational description 'the *x* such that *x* killed Caesar'. In other words, it is to confuse a killing and a thing that kills. Or, in general terms, a caus*ing* and a caus*er* or a cause. Davidson says, correctly, that 'my killing of the victim must be an action that results in the death of the victim'.[19] But resulting in is not the same as causing. How are they related? The answer is simple. Let 'A' be the name of an agent and let 'E' be the name of an event. 'The causing of E by A' is a nominalization of the sentence 'A caused E'; and the causing of E is the act which results in E.

The Queen's College, Oxford
UK
john.hyman@queens.ox.ac.uk

References

Alvarez, M. (1999). 'Actions and Events: some semantical considerations'. *Ratio* 12: 213–39.

Davidson, D. (1980a). 'Agency', in his *Essays on Actions and Events*. Oxford: Oxford University Press, 43–62.

Davidson, D. (1980b). 'The Individuation of Events', in his *Essays on Actions and Events*. Oxford: Oxford University Press, 163–180.

Davidson, D. (1985). 'Adverbs of Action', in B. Vermazen and M.B. Hintikka, eds, *Essays on Davidson*. Oxford: Oxford University Press, 230–241.

Hornsby, J. (1980). *Actions*. London: Routledge & Kegan Paul.

---

[19] Davidson 1980b, p. 178.

24   JOHN HYMAN

Kenny, A.J.P. (1963). *Action, Emotion and Will.* London: Routledge & Kegan Paul.
Lewis, D. (1980). 'Mad Pain and Martian Pain', in N. Block, ed., *Readings in the Philosophy of Psychology,* Vol. 1. London: Methuen, 216–222.
Parsons, T. (1990). *Events in the Semantics of English.* Cambridge, Mass.: MIT Press.
Prior, A.N. (1976). *The Doctrine of Propositions and Terms.* London: Duckworth.
Sellars, W. (1967). 'Rejoinder', in H.-N. Castañeda, ed., *Intentionality, Minds and Perception.* Detroit: Wayne University Press, 286–300.
Strawson, P.F. (1979). 'Perception and its Objects', in G.F. Macdonald, ed., *Perception and Identity.* London: Macmillan.
Williams, C.J.F. (1989). *What is Identity?* Oxford: Oxford University Press.

CHAPTER 3

LET THE VAT-BRAINS SPEAK FOR THEMSELVES

Gregory McCulloch

Abstract
It's pretty standard to find pretty compelling the claim that for all
one can tell one may be a vat-brain: not least, to say the least,
because it's a version of Descartes' demon thought-experiment in
the First Meditation. Here I refute that claim. Like Descartes I start
with the idea that one has an undeniable grip on most of what one
is thinking. To this I add the idea that knowing thinking as thinking is being able to engage in it. Then I argue that one can't
engage in the (purported) thinking of a vat-brain (there are various specimens of vat-brain to be considered). The essential point
is that one cannot make anything of what a vat-brain's intended
ontology would be, and how the brain might conceive of it. So one
cannot engage with any vat-brain's (purported) thinking. Yet one
engages with one's own. So one isn't any of them. I'm not, anyway:
you can speak for yourself.

I

My aim is to loosen very significantly the appeal of a very natural
thought: that for all I can tell maybe I'm a vat-brain.[1] But I need
to start by saying very briefly where I'm coming from. Some of my
assumptions are pretty controversial, but I (and others) have
argued for them elsewhere.

First, then, I go along with the likes of Descartes and Brentano
in holding that content or intentionality or world-directedness is
a feature of given conscious life, so that, for example, I can be
conscious that I am thinking *the cat is on the mat* in exactly the
same way I can be conscious that I feel an itch.[2] This has (rightly)

---

[1] Briefly, a vat-brain is a human brain kept in a vat of nutrients and stimulated by
inputs from a supercomputer (to which it outputs 'responses' so that e.g. it can replicate
the activity). This is very likely an impossible fiction but the idea can be used helpfully to
set up epistemological and other issues which have been traditional at least since
Descartes. For a clear description see Putnam 1981, ch. 1.

[2] See e.g. Strawson 1994, ch. 1. Also McCulloch 1995, ch. VI.

recently transmuted into an issue about first-person privilege:[3] but that's not my current concern.

Second, anyway, I don't follow Descartes in holding that what we thus know about our conscious life leaves us vulnerable to sceptical attack. In this case, the attack might go:

1. For all I can tell (albeit infallibly), maybe I'm a vat-brain; So,
2. I don't know much.

Of course, there are premisses missing and the conclusion is vague: and one task is to investigate whether there are believable candidates which would force (and sharpen) the conclusion. But my focus is different, since I'm going to attack premiss 1. And if I'm right, we can just forget about scepticism which assumes it. Put another way: my interest's in philosophy or metaphysics of mind, not epistemology.[4]

Third, I assume (with one small qualification to come later) that the default position is that if vat-brains are capable of conscious thought, then this conscious thought is directed at their electronic environment. If vat-brains think then, to use Putnam's phrase, they think about the vat-image in the computer. I take it (along with just about everyone else) that *this* much of externalism is right, because I reject the traditional Idea idea, along with just about everyone else. There are no such things as ideas as traditionally conceived, that is intrinsically contentful particulars that lurk inside brains or minds.[5]

Fourth, however, I assume that if we're to make sense of this suggestion that vat-brains think about their electronic environment, then we have to be able to share in this thinking, or replicate it on our own part. *Knowing thinking as such means doing it.* Understanding a thinker *as a thinker* means being able to interpret them. This is not a matter of having to believe what they believe, but it is a matter of being able to entertain their thoughts as *possible*, however curious, objects of belief.[6] With this in mind I'll sometimes focus on the idea of *communication*, which I here take to be a matter of mutual interpretation, a sharing of contents.

I'm going to argue that there's no such thing as the vat-image

[3] See Wright, Smith, Macdonald, eds, 1998.
[4] See McCulloch 1999a.
[5] See Wittgenstein, *Philosophical Investigations*, trans. G.E.M Anscombe 1953, passim.
[6] See McCulloch 1999b.

because we can't replicate it in our own minds. There is *no such thing* as interpreting these vat-brains. On the other hand, of course, I can perfectly well replicate my own thinking in my own mind. That's why I don't agree that for all I can tell, maybe I'm a vat-brain.

II

Those were the assumptions: now for some preliminaries. To do the whole job properly we need to be careful about the kind of vat-brain we're considering. Here are four different specimens:

vat-brain:1   An *ab initio* vat-brain in a largely empty universe.

vat-brain:2   An *ab initio* ongoing replica of vat-brain:1 in a largely empty universe but appropriately linked via computer to other *ab initio* vat-brains.

vat-brain:3   An *ab initio* ongoing replica of vat-brain:1 in the actual world.

vat-brain:4   An ongoing replica of vat-brain:1 which is the result of massive amputation on a person who was living a normal life in the actual world.

My principal focus here is on vat-brains 1 and 3, though I make a quick aside about vat-brain:2, and I shall round off with some comments about vat-brain:4. To make things graphic, and avoid needless controversy, I'll allow that our vat-brains process symbols of Mentalese, including ones I'll call CATs, which are reliably caused by C-type electronic impulses (CEIs).[7] Vat-brain:1 (hence all the others) is hereby stipulated to be an ongoing physical replica of my brain, so I also allow that *my* brain processes CATs (though these are reliably caused by cats). I've no idea whether this is true, but I can afford to concede it for the sake of this argument.

But: if we now call vat-brain:1's CATs *mental representations*, and think of intentionality (at least with respect to the material realm) in terms of reliable causation of mental representations, we can immediately conclude that vat-brain:1's CAT-processing is intentionally directed at CEIs, that it has CEI thoughts.

Just like that. It's that easy.

But if we do that, the question about vat-brain:1 has been begged at the outset. If this question isn't to be begged, the notion of *mental representation* has to be earned in its case. And

---

[7] See Fodor 1987.

whether it can be earned just is the matter at issue whether vat-brain:1 has conscious thoughts about its electronic environment. If you say that intentionality (where material things are concerned) = mental representation + reliable cause, then all the interesting issues are wrapped up in the idea of *what it is to be a mental representation*. Here it's also illicit to gesture towards the idea of a law-like correlation between the vat-brains' CATs, and the CEIs. The immediate question is whether such presumed lawlike correlations are psychological or psychophysical: and again this involves the matter at issue. And, of course, talk of the brains' 'virtual reality' is also *sub judice*, however natural it may be to resort to it. More generally, it's one thing to agree that part of the enabling mechanism for the mind contains CATs, another to say that any container of CATs *is* a mind, and that processes in this container are thus mental processes. Perhaps CATs can only correctly be called mental representations if they play the right sort of role in enabling the thinking and related activity of a thinking subject in touch with its environment. Then my CATs, we could perhaps allow, are mental representations and our question is *whether our vat-brains' are too*. And note that even if my CATs *are* mental representations, it doesn't follow that my brain, the container of these representations, is itself a thinker. This too is at least very close to the matter at issue.

I'm going to argue that the CATs of our vat-brains are not mental representations, and that the brains consequently have no 'virtual world'. But just to show that I want to tackle head-on the powerful intuitions that people have about the supposed consciousness of vat-brains, I shall adopt the following convention. Where I'm said to think that P or refer to Ts, I'll say that the vat-brains think that #P# or refer to #Ts#. So instead of saying 'the vat-brain's thought corresponding to my thought that cats eat mice' I'll say 'the vat-brain's thought that #cats eat mice#'; and instead of saying 'the vat-brain's virtual cats' I'll say 'the vat-brain's #cats#'. What we're going to see is that these conventions create, at best, a mere illusion of sense.

If this sounds surprising, that's because it can seem deceptively easy to picture to ourselves what it's like for these vat-brains, to imagine their conscious situation. For example, since I've stipulated that vat-brain:1 is an ongoing replica of my brain, it may seem easy for *me* to picture what it is like for vat-brain:1: it is like . . . THIS! But this suggestion trades on a massive illusion, the very same illusion we share when feeling the thrust of Descartes' demon scenario. It's also involved in Putnam's talk of 'the vat image', and it's what makes talk of the brain's 'virtual reality' so natural and compelling. But it's all illusory because imagining vat-brain:1's conscious life seems easy only so long as tacit reliance is placed on the traditional Idea idea, of intrinsically contentful items which bear their content or directedness-at on their face and can exist as they are independently of what's beyond them (cats or CEIs). For then we imagine that vat-brain:1 has such ideas in it which *match* the ones in mine, and we think we know what 'match' means here because we have seen matching pictures or photographs. But there are no such things as ideas in this sense. In other words, we have to *work very hard* to get a grip on what vat-brain:1's supposed conscious thinking about CEIs could be like, and hence on what sharing it would amount to. We can't just help ourselves to easy talk about #cats# and so on, thinking it quite clear what we mean.

III

Those were the assumptions and preliminaries, and I turn now to vat-brain:1 (an *ab initio* vat-brain in a largely empty universe). Suppose for the moment that there is no problem about its putative electronic ontology. Then it might seem easy enough to 'interpret' the CATs in vat-brain:1 by assigning them relevant elements from the ontology, namely the CEIs. Do this across the board, add a story of how the ways in which the symbols are hosted map on to types of propositional attitude, and won't the job be done?

No.

This is another massive and, I suspect, rather common illusion. *Of course* we can 'interpret' vat-brain:1's CATs in this sense (still assuming no problem with the ontology), just as we can so interpret any system of symbols (and much else) which are or can be systematically related to an environment or domain. But this is not yet to be in a position to ascribe conscious thinking to the symbols or their vehicle or system: obviously not in the general case, and *a fortiori* not in vat-brain:1's case.

Well then, let's fix up vat-brain:1 with a link through its computer to a screen on which it can flash messages according to its output. Or give it an amplifier and loudspeaker if you like. Since it's an ongoing replica of my brain, one might then suppose it to flash on to its screen or output through the loudspeaker just the sentences I utter, as and when I do. Then we can imagine parallel 'conversations' between myself and an interlocutor, and vat-brain:1 and my interlocutor's *Doppelganger* (imagine she has an appropriate input facility). Will not successful communication take place in vat-brain:1's case iff it does in mine? Will not my interlocutor's *Doppelganger* interpret vat-brain:1 to just the extent that my interlocutor interprets me?

Of course not. In making vat-brain:1 output sentences of English we're already on the way to rigging the matter in a very naive way. Why not arrange for it to output Chinese characters, or bar-codes? It's no reply to claim that in so far as it is conscious of #speaking# it will be conscious of English words. What, if anything, it's conscious of are #English words# in the computer, and we have yet to work out what, if anything, this consciousness could amount to. But let's let it have its English sentences. There's still a problem if my interlocutor's *Doppelganger* takes vat-brain:1's messages as utterances of English, and so construes the brain as expressing thoughts about cats just when I am. Even if vat-brain:1 is *uttering* in English, it certainly isn't *thinking* in English. If it has thoughts directed at anything at all, they're directed at CEIs and the like, and it's at best merely using the English words that we've given it to utter about these. And while we might, as before, 'interpret' this output using the putative electronic ontology, this will not, as before, get us as far as entitlement to ascribe conscious thought to the source of the output. In itself, the fact that these symbols – the ones on the screen or coming out of the loudspeaker – are outside vat-brain:1 rather than inside it makes no relevant difference.

So what more needs to be done? Here we should first note that part of what it means to say that intentionality characterises consciousness is that in conscious thought (as in thought generally) objects are presented to the mind under this or that guise, as such and such a thing (and of course the same thing can be presented under more than one guise).[8] My interlocutor's *Doppelganger*, then, will somehow have to latch on to the ways in which CEIs are presented to vat-brain:1 (if they are): will have to share its ways-of-thinking-about CEIs and other electronic impulses. Having done this, she will then be able to replicate in her own mind the vat-brain's putative thinking about CEIs, and

---

[8]   Thus, of course, Frege, 'On *Sinn* and *Bedeutung*', in Beaney 1997.

get some way towards understanding what it's like to be the vat-brain (if it's like anything).

Things are not as straightforward as they may seem, however, and we can start to see this by noting some of the problems that would stand in the way of successful communication between my interlocutor's *Doppelganger* and vat-brain:1. First, as long as my interlocutor's *Doppelganger* continued to input words of English *meant as such*, there would be at least one-way communication breakdown: her utterances would be about cats but would be taken, by vat-brain:1 – if taken at all – as being about CEIs. So, obviously, my interlocutor's *Doppelganger* needs to learn Vatese, and talk about the electronic environment. Then in doing this she would be in a position also to put the correct interpretation on vat-brain:1's output.

But could anything count as my interlocutor's *Doppelganger* coming to understand Vatese, given that this would involve getting her mind around CEIs etc. *as these are (allegedly) presented to vat-brain:1*? There are two very severe problems here. First, it's very unclear whether vat-brain:1 could even think about CEIs as a certain kind of *electronic impulse*, since it's dubious that one could have such a concept without a fair amount of physical theory and the like. And vat-brain:1 could have no physical theory. Corresponding to our fundamental category of *physical object* it would have (one tries to say) *electronic impulse* or, less incoherently, something else entirely – #physical object# – which just happens to latch on to what we know as electronic impulses. But what does vat-brain:1 know them as? We've no way of saying, no way of beginning to imagine how vat-brain:1 could conceive of its fundamental ontology, unless we attribute to it, indefensibly I say, the concept *electronic impulse*. That's the first problem.

The second is that even if we generously ignore this, we are still left clueless over how the elements of the ontology would *individually* present themselves to vat-brain:1's supposed consciousness. Under what guise do electronic impulses present themselves to vat-brain:1? What kind of electronic impulse would they strike it as (given the very generous thought that they strike it as *some* kind of electronic impulse)? What's the difference between CEIs and DEIs (its #dogs#), from vat-brain:1's point of view?

The overwhelmingly natural reply here is 'vat-brain:1's CEIs are presented as cats', or perhaps 'they present themselves to vat-brain:1 in the way that cats present themselves to GMcC' (recall they're all ongoing replicas of my brain): and once again, it's equally natural and tempting to lapse into talk of the brain's #cats# or 'virtual cats', and the like. But all of this is just to revert *uncritically* to the view dismissed earlier, that vat-brain:1's alleged consciousness in some way 'matches' my own. The likely culprit here, also dismissed already, is the background influence of the Idea idea. But another possible culprit, I suspect, is a watered-down version, or vestige, of this, something like the claim that thinking, *in so far as it is present to consciousness,* supervenes on brain activity. But this claim is ruled out by the conjunction of my first assumption – content *itself* is given to consciousness – and my third assumption – content doesn't supervene on brain activity.

IV

Overall, then, we have and can attain no idea at all what, if anything, we express when we write the likes of '#the cat is on the mat#', at least where vat-brain:1 is concerned. I take it that that certainly does start to loosen the appeal of the thought that for all I can tell, maybe I'm a vat-brain. I now want to consider vat-brain:3 (an *ab initio* ongoing replica of vat-brain:1 in the actual world): and by way of preliminary I'll make my promised aside involving vat-brain:2 (an *ab initio* ongoing replica of vat-brain:1 in a largely empty universe but appropriately linked via computer to other *ab initio* vat-brains).

And as a preliminary to *this,* note first that my interlocutor's *Doppelganger* doesn't exist in vat-brain:1's world. Pretending for the moment that vat-brain:1 has some thoughts and experiences directed at its #partner# in the putative conversation (#the other speaker#), this #partner# would have to be an aspect of vat-brain:1's (electronic) environment, like all the other objects of its thinking. Just as its CATs are directed at CEIs, its DOGS at DEIs, so its SPEAKERs would be directed at SEIs. So it doesn't matter at all whether my interlocutor's *Doppelganger* intends her inputs as English, Vatese, or nothing. It makes no difference to vat-brain:1 what happens 'beyond' its electronic environment: that is all noumenal.[9] Thus there is no question of real communication, of any meaningful contact or meeting of minds at all, in the input direction. My interlocutor's *Doppelganger* is beyond the cognitive reach of vat-brain:1.

---

[9] Compare here McDowell 1994 in note 14, p. 17. For a mildly critical discussion of McDowell's claims in the attached text, see McCulloch (forthcoming).

Note now that second, things are no different in the case of vat-brain:2, hooked up to one or more other vat-brains through an appropriate computer link, with relevant harmonies established.[10] None of these vat-brains would be in the world of any other, and solipsism (or the appropriate version of it, #solipsism#, if there is such a thing) would be the *correct* position for the likes of vat-brain:2. This goes even if we can so arrange it that the CATs of vat-brain:2 and its 'cohorts' are caused by the *same* CEIs. For even though the brains would thus have overlapping ontologies, still no vat-brain would be in the ontology of any other, and Putnam's supposition that there could be a 'speech'-community of vat-brains is thus something of a sham.

It is facile to suppose that these solipsistic vat-brains could somehow get to a conception of the Others by adopting #an inference to the best explanation# of their #conversational# experience. In supposing them to have conscious thinking directed at their world, including #the other speakers#, we have not obviously left any room for the idea that something needs to be explained by them. #Others# would be right there in front of them, just like #cats#! Anyway, a thinker can only go through an inference *P, so Q* if it has all the concepts involved, and this in turn means that the objects presented by these concepts will be in the thinker's ontology (remember my third assumption of mild externalism, which nearly everyone, including lovers of vat-brains, goes along with). But the present idea is that our vat-brains have an electronic ontology (if any). So the vat-brain's attempt to #quantify# along the lines of #there is something 'behind' this body which is the real Other# will only come out appropriately true if the other vat-brains are already in its ontology to be #quantified over#. And this has been ruled out by stipulation.

Or to put the matter otherwise, the challenge here for anyone wanting to avoid the solipsistic result for our vat-brains is to provide a principled, non-question-begging reason why their environment should be *stretched* to include non-electronic elements, such as other vat-brains or things like my interlocutor's *Doppel-ganger*. And this idea of 'stretching' the environment is important in the context of vat-brain:3 and vat-brain:4, as we'll now see.

---

[10] Putnam 1981, ch. 1.

V

The salient issue with vat-brain:3 is that although it is *ab initio,* it's in *this* world, rather than vat-brain:1's largely empty universe. So we've the option of 'stretching' its environment to embrace the cats and other worldly things beyond its CEIs. At a pinch, we could even arrange for its stretched environment to be an ongoing replica of my own, so that in keeping vat-brain:3 in step with my brain the computer would be keeping vat-brain:3's brain activity as appropriate to its (stretched) environment as mine is to my actual environment. Someone might then claim that vat-brain:3 is having veridical hallucinations of its stretched environment.

I say that these would be hallucinations at best because I'm not (yet) supposing that there's any causal interaction between vat-brain:3 and the elements of its stretched environment. The case presently under consideration is one where vat-brain:3's situation is parallel to vat-brain:1's, except that in the former case, but not the latter, there's the actual world beyond the electronic environment (although, to repeat, vat-brain:3 is causally insulated from it).

What's the dialectical situation here? Is the onus on me to say why vat-brain:3 isn't hallucinating cats and the like, or is the onus rather on the opposition to argue that it is? Given what has been said about vat-brain:1, it's blindingly obvious that the onus is on the opposition. What, apart from wishful thinking, is the motivation for stretching vat-brain:3's environment? For the question is begged if we now suppose it unproblematic that vat-brain:3 has a conscious life which appropriately 'matches' mine (and hence tracks the stretched environment as much as mine does). Why should its conscious life match mine rather than vat-brain:1's alleged conscious life? In fact, there is much more reason for saying the latter than the former, given that vat-brain:3 is causally insulated from the elements of its stretched environment. Its situation is not materially any different from vat-brain:1's: its CATs are caused by CEIs, its SPEAKERs by SEIs, and so on. But if so, and vat-brain:3's conscious life 'matches' vat-brain:1's, then we have no conception of what, if anything, it's like. Hence we can't suppose it has hallucinatory experience of the stretched environment.

Things begin to get more complicated once the causal insulation starts to break down. Of course, it can do so progressively, as in the above case where we imagined my interlocutor's *Doppelganger* causally interacting with vat-brain:1. But let's first imagine a less loaded case of what I'll call *partial stretching.*

Suppose we break the causal insulation between vat-brain:3's computer and *just* the cats in the wider world: say we fit it with an appropriate cat-detector, so that cats now cause (most of) the CEIs which in turn cause vat-brain:3's CATs (cats will cause all of those CEIs which cause CATs which correspond to my CATs which are (appropriately) caused by cats). Does this causal correlation give any reason to conclude that vat-brain:3 can now at least think about cats?

Not really.

Suppose it can think about cats. Then it might seem that we can start to interpret at least some of vat-brain:3's alleged thinking, as when I think 'The cat's on the mat' and vat-brain:3 goes through the same motions as my brain. But, of course, it's not true that vat-brain:3 thereby thinks that *the cat is on the mat*: rather, what (at best) it thinks is that #*the*# cat #*is on the mat*#. And here we still have no clue as to what, if anything, vat-brain:3 is thinking about our cat, since its MATs are caused by MEIs, and we don't have a clue how, if at all, these strike vat-brain:3 (let's not even try to go into the issue of the other words involved). In fact, we're not doing vat-brain:3 any favours at all by stretching its environment to include cats. '#The# cat #is on the mat#' is at best false (the Vatese 'is on the mat' applies to electronic impulses which stand in certain relations (#relations#?) to other electronic impulses), and is at worse nonsense, a sort of category mistake. But – we can stipulate (pretend) – the thought that #the cat is on the mat# is perfectly correct given vat-brain:3's (alleged) #circumstances#, since it marches in step with my brain, and my 'The cat is on the mat' is beyond reproach. So by stretching vat-brain:3's environment we put it more in the wrong than it would otherwise be. Charity dictates no partial stretching!

Now I've no wish or need to be charitable here. But things are otherwise for lovers of vat-brains. . .

To a certain extent the above considerations carry over to other speakers, such as my interlocutor's *Doppelganger*. She is, after all, a real-worldly object like the cats, and an argument parallel to the one just given, concerning my utterance of 'the other speaker's on the mat', would conclude that charity dictates no partial stretching. But here there's a complication, since charity would then also thus dictate that vat-brain:3 would be a #solipsist# and that its alleged conscious life is beyond our ken. And wouldn't it be better (more charitable) to avoid these things by foisting the likes of #the other# speaker #is on the mat# on vat-brain:3?

No.

Relative to its having the unstretched, electronic environment which charity would *ceteris paribus* assign it, #solipsism# is the *correct* position for vat-brain:3 to adopt: so there's no lack of charity here. Nor does it seem on balance uncharitable to conclude that vat-brain:3's conscious thinking is, if anything, beyond our ken. It may be an unwelcome conclusion for lovers of vat-brains to have to confront, but that's quite another matter. True, certain thoughts had by vat-brains confronting interlocutors would come out false (#well, we certainly saw eye to eye there#), but this is to be set against the probable nonsense ascribed under partial stretching (#the other# speaker #is on the mat#). Indeed, in so far as charity dictates maximising sense rather than truth, it would seem still that partial stretching is the less charitable of the two options.

Partial stretching thus has nothing going for it. Those of us who hate vat-brains see no motivation to stretch, those who love vat-brains have a motivation (charity) not to.

So what if we go further, and so arrange things that *all* of the (appropriate) symbols processed by vat-brain:3 are caused, *via* the mediation of the computer, by elements of the actual world? Let's give vat-brain:3 the necessary receptors (while it is #asleep#). Now it may seem that there is no impediment to ascribing the thought that the cat is on the mat in appropriate circumstances to vat-brain:3: if anything, one could argue that charity would rather suggest one should.

Prospects for this are not so good, however.

First, in so far as attention remains on vat-brain:3's putative thinking about its surroundings, stretched or otherwise, charity is impotent. By hypothesis, vat-brain:3's putative thinking is as appropriate to its electronic environment as my thinking is to my real environment. So here stretching brings no gain, and the suspicion remains that it's motivated solely by wishful thinking or cussedness. Second, this is confirmed when we direct attention to vat-brain:3's supposed conception of its own situatedness in its surroundings. Since it marches in step with my brain, it will have #a body#, and will #interact with and perform actions on the things it lives among#. And in its own view (if there is one) these matters will hang together as smoothly as do the corresponding matters involving me in *my* view. But since, by hypothesis, we have not supplied vat-brain:3 with a body or with any other way to intervene in the real world, stretching will tend to make garbled nonsense of its own (putative) view of itself. Thus when I think 'My legs are getting pretty tired as a result of walking up this hill' vat-brain:3, under stretching, will be ascribed #My legs are getting pretty tired as a result of walking up this# hill. And so on. Once again, charity forbids stretching, even given *total* breakdown of the causal insulation between vat-brain:3 and the actual world.

Well then, let's go the whole hog and equip not only vat-brain:3's computer with all the necessary *detectors*, but also equip the package of vat-brain:3 + computer with the wherewithal to intervene appropriately in the stretched environment. Give it a *body*, and call the whole assembly Jerry. Now when

(1) I think *the cat is on the mat* and consequently reach out to flip it off;

and

(2) vat-brain:1 (putatively) thinks #the cat is on the mat# and consequently (putatively at least seems to itself to) #reach out to flip it off#;

what happens in the case of vat-brain:3? As a first stab at what is not too contentious:

(3) vat-brain:3 **either** (putatively) thinks #the cat is on the mat# **or** (really) thinks the cat is on the mat;

and

(4) Jerry reaches out to flip it off.

But given the appropriateness of Jerry's engagement with the stretched environment, one might think it overwhelmingly plausible to insist on the second disjunct of (3), namely

(5) vat-brain:3 (really) thinks the cat is on the mat,

because vat-brain:3 is *obviously* now a fully paid-up thinker about the actual environment.

This is no good.

The *most* we are forced to accept here is that *Jerry* is a fully paid-up thinker about the actual environment, so that

(6) Jerry (really) thinks the cat is on the mat.

And we can concede that, for the sake of argument: in making Jerry we make a thinker. But it doesn't follow, from the fact that Jerry is a thinker, even that the package of *vat-brain:3 + computer* is a thinker, much less that vat-brain:3 is. In effect, the package would be serving as Jerry's brain or cognitive enabler. But it no more follows that if Jerry thinks, his enabler thinks, than it follows that if I think, my enabler thinks. Or perhaps better: these entailments can't be assumed here, since we're in the midst of an argument which bears crucially on whether they hold.

In fact, it's probably anyway only wishful thinking on the part of lovers of vat-brains to say that Jerry is a thinker. Another description of the example is that Jerry is a puppet which is pushed around the real world thanks to the outputs from vat-brain:3's computer, alongside which vat-brain:3 continues, as ever (allegedly), blissfully secure in its electronic environment. Presumably the matter depends on, among other things, how the outputs control the behaviour. Or perhaps we have two candidate thinkers here with different ontologies: Jerry/real world, vat-brain:3/computer. But however all that may be, it seems that if you really do start off with a fully paid-up thinker in its virtual world, that's what you end up with, regardless of how you tinker with the noumenal surroundings. From *our* point of view – or at least from the point of view of lovers of vat-brains – this tinkering may seem to make all the difference in the world. But surely things are otherwise from the most important perspective of all: the (putative) point of view of the vat-brain itself. A noumenon is a noumenon is a noumenon, and these reflections on sensitive interpretative practice drive this home.

Overall, then, the proposal to stretch vat-brain:3's environment is uncharitable and/or unmotivated and/or question-begging, and I submit that we should say the same about vat-brain:3's putative conscious thinking as we say about vat-brain1:'s. Namely, that we have no idea what, if anything, it amounts to. And I take it that this loosens even further the appeal of the thought that for all I can tell, maybe I'm a vat-brain.

VI

I turn finally to vat-brain:4, which presents a different kind of challenge. Since it has been taken from the body of a person who has lived a normal life in the actual world, there is the possibility that this history has equipped vat-brain:4 with the concepts necessary for conscious thought about cats, etc. This in turn leaves the possibility that it could carry these intentional properties with it into the vat.

In fact it's moot whether this possibility can be pressed without the begging of crucial questions – it's close to assuming that brains are thinkers – and I've anyway elsewhere independently argued that states of a person's brain are not the bearers of the person's contents.[11] But let's ignore all this in a spirit of exploration.

Note that in making this concession I do weaken somewhat my case against the idea that for all I can tell, maybe I'm a vat-brain: since I at least leave it open that maybe I'm a *recently envatted* brain. However, for reasons I cannot go into now, I don't think that this qualified claim has the potential to generate a sceptical challenge as powerful or as principled as that threatened by the unqualified claim:[12] and anyway, to repeat, I am only allowing it in a spirit of exploration.

Vat-brain:4 could be relocated into the situation imagined earlier for vat-brain:3. That is, it could be placed in (though kept causally insulated from) surroundings which replicate mine, so that its computer, in keeping it in step with my brain, would ensure that vat-brain:4's brain activity would be as appropriate to its (stretched) environment as mine is to mine. If the brain carries intentional properties into the vat, there would then be a very good *prima facie* case for saying that it had veridical hallucinations of its stretched environment: a much better case than in the parallel situation involving vat-brain:3.

To make progress, let's first imagine a different case, in which God destroys most of the universe after His disembodying of vat-brain:4. Vat-brain:4 would then be in the same boat or largely empty universe as vat-brain:1 at least as far as its supposed present-tensed thinking is concerned, and what we now seem to have is a situation corresponding somewhat to the switching cases discussed with reference to Twin Earth. That is, over time, vat-brain:4's CATs, previously caused by cats (when it was embodied), would come to be reliably caused by CEIs, and the same would hold, *mutatis mutandis*, for its other symbols which were previously caused by worldly things. Then, very plausibly, vat-brain:4's supposed mental life would start to fade into one parallel with vat-brain:1's, since the constant ongoing interaction with CEIs would shift the reference of its CATs. But since we have no idea what, if anything, vat-brain:1's conscious thinking amounts to, we'd have

---

[11] McCulloch 1995, chs IV–VIII; compare McCulloch 1998.
[12] See McCulloch 1999a.

to conclude that vat-brain:4's conscious life, even if it still has one straight after the switch, would fade after a decent spell in the vat into either nothing or at best something unknowable by us. Note that I've not had to legislate on whether it carries any intentional properties with it into the vat. All that's needed is the earlier result about vat-brain:1, and the point about reference shift in the case of vat-brain:4.

We're now in a position to go back to the straight vat-brain:4 case, where God doesn't destroy anything after envatting vat-brain:4. As long as vat-brain:4 is kept causally insulated from the world beyond the computer, the same point about fade-out will come up here, where vat-brain:4's situation after the disembodiment replicates vat-brain:3's. For we have already seen that if vat-brain:3 is thinking at all then it is doing so in an inscrutable way about CEIs, rather than about the cats in its stretched environment (from the elements of which it is causally insulated). Then vat-brain:4's immediately post-disembodiment mental life, assuming it has one, would gradually fade into this, even in the case where God does not destroy most of the stretched environment. So once again, such grip as we start with on vat-brain:4's conscious thinking rapidly weakens in the now familiar way.

What if the causal insulation is broken down? If it's partial, then we'd have partial fade-out and consequent garbling (#the# cat #sat on the mat#), and charity dictates not stretching. If the breakdown is complete but no new body is supplied, fade-out occurs with respect to all of vat-brain:4's alleged consciousness of its own dealings with the world (#My legs are getting pretty tired as a result of walking up this# hill), and once again charity – sympathy for not the devil but the brain's own supposed view of itself and its place in its world – would dictate total fade-out.

What if the package of vat-brain:4 + computer is fitted with a body, call the resulting ensemble Terry?

If this is done after the brain has been in the vat long enough for fade-out to have occurred, then we can describe Terry just as we described Jerry, and vat-brain:4 would be *at best* a solipsistic inscrutable thinker which happens to be part of the cognitive enabler of another thinker, Terry.

If the embodying is done before fade-out – say the brain is robbed of its body and immediately attached to a computer which is embedded in a body, call the resulting ensemble Perry – then what?

First, perhaps depending on the empirical details, we might

consider this to be no different from transplanting the brain from one body to another: it's just that Perry's body incorporates a supercomputer. Then the brain isn't really in a vat anyway and all bets are off. The computer is just an extension of its new nervous system. And it no more follows from the fact that Perry is a thinker that the package of brain + computer is a thinker, than it follows from the fact that I am a thinker that my brain is a thinker. Much less does it follow that the transplanted brain would be a thinker.

But, second, we might consider this to be a genuine transfer of the brain to a vat: perhaps because the links between the body and the computer output are unsuitable for allowing the package of brain + computer to serve as Perry's cognitive enabler. Here, I say, reference-shift and hence fade-out would happen, and the body and the actual world would thus go noumenal after a decent length of time. For if it really is the case that brain + computer is not linked to the host body so as to serve as Perry's cognitive enabler, then how could these links be such as to underwrite intentional relations to the body's environment? If the outputs cannot subserve intentional action how can the inputs subserve perception?

So: there's no real appeal in the thought that for all I can tell, maybe I'm a vat-brain. Your move.[13]

Philosophy Department
University of Birmingham
Edgbaston
Birmingham B15 2TT
UK

[13] Earlier versions of this material were delivered at Cambridge, Dubrovnik, Glasgow, Hertfordshire, Lampeter and Swansea, as well as the Reading Conference on *Meaning and Representation*, 2000: I'm grateful to the organisers for inviting me and thus giving me a reason to get to work. Many comments from members of the audiences helped me to refine it: I recall a particularly searching examination from Jim Edwards and Philip Percival in Glasgow; spending what seemed like the whole night trying to fend off a pack of wild dogs in Cambridge at the Moral Science Club; and getting gently but firmly disbelieved in Lampeter. I've inflicted it on my colleagues in Birmingham more times than I should have, but it was always so beneficial. Finally thanks to Jerry Fodor for his polite and forbearing remarks at the Reading conference.

References

Fodor, J. (1987). *Psychosemantics*. Cambridge, Mass.: MIT Press.

Frege, G. (1997). 'On *Sinn* and *Bedeutung*', in M. Beaney, ed., *The Frege Reader*. Oxford: Blackwell.

McCulloch, G. (1995). *The Mind and its World*. London: Routledge & Kegan Paul.

McCulloch, G. (1998). 'Intentionality and Interpretation', in A. O'Hear, ed, *Current Issues in the Philosophy of Mind* (*Philosophy* Supplement 43). Cambridge: Cambridge University Press, 253–71.

McCulloch, G. (1999a). 'Content Externalism and Cartesian Scepticism', in R. Sterne, ed., *Transcendental Arguments*. Oxford: Clarendon Press, 251–270.

McCulloch, G. (1999b). 'From Quine to the Epistemological Real Distinction'. *European Journal of Philosophy* 7, 30–46.

McCulloch, G. (forthcoming). 'Phenomenological Externalism', in N. Smith, ed, *Reading McDowell: On Mind and World*. London: Routledge.

McDowell, J. (1994). *Mind and World*. Cambridge, Mass.: Harvard University Press.

Putnam, H. (1981). *Reason, Truth and History*. Cambridge: Cambridge University Press.

Strawson, G. (1994). *Mental Reality*. Cambridge, Mass.: MIT Press.

Wittgenstein, L. (1953). *Philosophical Investigations*, trans. G.E.M. Anscombe. Oxford: Blackwell.

Wright, C., B.C. Smith, and C. Macdonald, eds, (1998). *Knowing Our Own Minds*. Oxford: Clarendon Press.

CHAPTER 4

INTENTIONAL OBJECTS[1]

Tim Crane

Abstract
The idea of an intentional object, or an object of thought, gives rise to a dilemma for theories of intentionality. Either intentional objects are existing objects, in which case it is impossible, contrary to appearances, to think about something which does not exist. Or some intentional objects are non-existent real objects. But this requires an obscure and implausible metaphysics. I argue that the way out of this dilemma is to deny that being an intentional object is being an entity of any kind. 'Object' here does not mean *thing* or *entity*. Rather, to say that something is an intentional object is just to say that it is an object of thought (or other intentional state or act) for a subject. It is further argued that theories of intentionality should not dispense with the idea of an intentional object.

Is there, or should there be, any place in contemporary philosophy of mind for the concept of an intentional object? Many philosophers would make short work of this question. In a discussion of what intentional objects are supposed to be, John Searle's answer to our question is brisk and dismissive:

> an Intentional object is just an object like any other; it has no peculiar ontological status at all. To call something an Intentional object is just to say that it is what some intentional state is about. Thus, for example, if Bill admires President Carter, then the Intentional object of his admiration is President Carter, the actual man and not some shadowy intermediate entity between Bill and the man.[2]

The last claim expressed here seems obviously correct. For on the

---

[1] I am grateful to Katalin Farkas, Paul Horwich, Greg McCulloch, David Smith, Jerry Valberg and the participants at the Reading conference on *Meaning and Representation* in April 2000, for discussion of the issues raised in this paper.
[2] Searle 1983.

face of it, Bill's admiration of President Carter makes direct contact with the man himself; Bill does not first admire something else – some mental or non-mental 'intermediary' – and in virtue of admiring this thing, he admires President Carter. This makes little phenomenological or metaphysical sense, and there is no particular reason to believe it. We should surely join Searle, then, in rejecting 'shadowy intermediaries' in thought.

But the rest of this passage of Searle's, it seems to me, is problematic. For one thing, it is in need of an obvious and simple clarification, since as it stands it cannot be true. But even once this clarification is made, Searle's claim entails an absurdity when combined with a familiar and recalcitrant fact about intentionality: that intentional states can be about things which do not exist. I will make the clarification first, and then bring out the absurdity.

In elaborating his claim about intentional objects, Searle says that intentional objects are 'ordinary objects'.[3] If he means by 'object' what is usually meant when we contrast objects with *properties, relations, events, propositions, facts* or *states of affairs* – that is, particular objects – then the claim that all intentional objects (defined above as 'what some intentional state is about') are objects in this sense is simply false. Intentional states can be about events, properties and all things in all the ontological categories just mentioned. There is no reason to think that the only things our intentional states are about are particular objects in the ordinary sense. So Searle cannot mean *object* in this sense; he must rather mean something like *ordinary existing thing* or *entity* (where *thing* or *entity* is the most general ontological category: properties, relations and so on are all things or entities). So now the claim that intentional objects are ordinary *objects* just means that what intentional states are about are ordinary existing *entities*.[4]

But once we make this clarification, and once we bring into play the idea that intentional states can be about things which do not exist, then the absurdity of Searle's claim comes to the surface. For consider the conjunction of Searle's two claims with this idea:

(1) Intentional objects are ordinary existing entities.
(2) Intentional objects are what intentional states are about.
(3) Intentional states can be about things which do not exist.

3 *Ibid.*, p. 18.
4 Cf. Martin 1998, p. 101.

It follows from (1)–(3) that some ordinary existing entities do not exist, which is absurd, and clearly not what Searle has in mind. It might be thought that the way to respond is to drop 'existing' in (1), but the conclusion that some ordinary entities do not exist is only superficially less absurd. If there are entities which do not exist, then they hardly deserve to be called ordinary.

What has gone wrong? It seems that (1)–(3) cannot be true together; but which of them is false? Claim (2) is simply a definition and so cannot be sensibly debated. But is (3) true? It is certainly hard to deny. Consider a debate between an atheist and a theist, and suppose for the sake of argument that the atheist is right: God does not exist. (Let's suppose that the debate they are having is a straightforward one over the existence of the Christian God as traditionally conceived: the all-powerful creator of the universe who loves us as a father loves his children etc.) If the atheist is right, then the theist has been talking about (and thinking about) something which does not exist. Yet the theist's words made sense, it seemed that he was able to put these thoughts about God into words. His thoughts are thoughts about something that does not exist. Or consider H.H. Price, hallucinating a pile of leaves on his counterpane under the influence of mescaline.[5] If Price thought 'That pile of leaves wasn't there this morning' then he was thinking about something which does not exist: there is no pile of leaves. And there are many other kinds of examples: from myth and fiction (Pegasus), the history of science (Phlogiston, Vulcan), and from the experience of after-images and double vision etc. Even if you thought you could explain away some of these examples without appealing to the idea of 'thinking about something which does not exist', the prospect of explaining all of them away seems unpromising.

So the initial simple plausibility of (1) is misleading; given (2) and (3), it seems that we should abandon it. If we do, then it may seem too that we need a *theory* of the special nature of these intentional objects. In appealing to intentional objects in giving an account of perceptual experience, Gilbert Harman admits that he has no 'fully worked-out account' of intentional objects – implying that this is what is needed for a proper account of perceptual intentionality. Harman agrees that it is no solution to say that intentional objects are *mental* objects (or at any rate, that not all of them are). When Ponce de Leon looked for the

---

[5] The story is referred to by Anscombe 1965.

Fountain of Youth, he was not looking for something in his (or anyone else's) mind. So however the final theory of intentional objects turns out, it 'had better end up agreeing that Ponce de Leon was looking for something when he was looking for the Fountain of Youth, even though there is no Fountain of Youth, and the theory had better *not* have the consequence that Ponce de Leon was looking for something mental'.[6]

But if intentional objects are not mental objects, what are they? If we accept (2) and (3), then on the face of it we must accept that some intentional objects do not exist. So we need a theory of non-existent objects or entities. (Harman himself mentions Terence Parsons' theory.[7]) According to such theories, the things which exist do not exhaust all the things that there are; for there are many things which do not exist. Of all the things we think about, some of them (like Carter) exist, and some of them (like Pegasus) do not. It could be said that Pegasus has being, but he does not exist. And if we can think about impossible objects, then there are these things too. They necessarily do not exist. It cannot be an objection to this theory that it denies Quine's view that the English quantifier 'There are. . .' expresses existence (so that 'There are things which do not exist' is a contradiction) since the theory is explicitly proposed in opposition to the Quinean orthodoxy.[8]

But it seems to me that such a theory is fraught with problems. How are we supposed to understand the distinction between being and existence? Specifying two domains of quantification, one a subset of the other, is not enough by itself, since what we need to understand is what distinguishes the things in the subclass (the existent) from the things in the broader class (the entities, things which have being). Moreover, the nature of the postulated entities is obscure. On the face of it, we do not have any idea of what makes it the case that two people are thinking about the same non-existent object. Indeed, intentional objects can be indeterminate, even in a sense that vague objects (if there are such things) never are. As G.E.M. Anscombe puts it,

> I can think of a man without thinking of a man of any particular height; I cannot hit a man without hitting a man of any

---

[6] Harman 1990; reprinted in Block, Owen and Flanagan, eds, 1997, p. 666. I should add that Harman does not commit himself to the theory of non-existent objects. As he says: 'I am quite willing to believe that there are not really any nonexistent objects and that apparent talk of such objects should be analysed away somehow'.

[7] Parsons 1980.

[8] See Quine 1953.

particular height, because there is no such thing as a man of no particular height.[9]

So we need to understand not just the idea of objects which do not exist, but also the fact that they can be indeterminate in this way. But what sense can be made of an indeterminate object? The man who is of no particular height: what colour is his hair? No particular colour? But that surely means: no colour at all. And how can anything have hair without that hair being any colour at all? Is this just an expression of our 'prejudice in favour of the existent', that something which has hair has hair of some particular colour? But what is the real alternative to this prejudice? The view, as far as I can see, offers no real answer to these questions.

What has emerged is a dilemma: either deny that intentional states can be about things that do not exist, or accept that there are non-existent objects. Neither position is acceptable. The way out of the dilemma is to reject an assumption shared by both unacceptable positions: that *to be an intentional object is to be a thing or entity of a certain kind*. The position which denies (3) assumes that intentional objects are just existing entities. The position which postulates non-existent objects assumes that all intentional objects are entities, although some of them are non-existent ones. The common assumption is that to be an intentional object is to be an entity. This is what I shall deny.

This might sound perverse or paradoxical. If I am thinking about Carter, Carter is the intentional object of my thought. Yet Carter exists, he is an entity. So how can I deny that some intentional objects actually are entities? I do not deny this: this is just another way of saying that some intentional objects exist and some do not. What I am denying is that *being an intentional object as such* is *being an entity* of any kind.

The basis of this view is a proper understanding of what an *object* is in this context. We use the term 'object' in a number of different ways, and some of these ways are very different from others. One is when we talk about physical objects. Here the word can be replaced by 'thing': my computer is a physical object; therefore it is a physical thing. Interestingly the converse is not true: if x is a physical thing, it's not always true that x is a physical object. It makes sense to say that gravity is a physical thing; but not that it is a physical object. Someone who says that

[9] Anscombe 1965, p. 161.

love is a physical thing is not thereby committed to its being a physical object. This supports my suggestion above that 'thing' picks out a more general ontological category than 'object'. So all physical objects are physical things, but not all physical things are physical objects. Contrast the phrases 'object of attention' or 'object of experience'. As J.J. Valberg has pointed out, we cannot replace the word 'object' in these phrases with the word 'thing' and retain sense: 'thing of attention' and 'thing of experience' make no sense.[10] The word 'object' has a different meaning in these phrases than it does in the phrases 'physical object', 'material object', 'mental object' and even 'abstract object'. This is the key to the idea that being an intentional object is not being a thing of any kind. For 'intentional object' in this respect (unsurprisingly) is like 'object of attention' rather than 'physical object'. If it makes sense at all, 'intentional thing' means the same as 'intentional entity', which someone might take to mean *intensional entity*, in the sense in which propositions and other intensions are intensional entities. Whatever the merits of the view that there are intensional entities, such entities are plainly not what is meant by talking of intentional objects. When I consider my cat Jeffrey, it is the cat which is the object of my thought, the thing I am thinking about. I am not thinking about an intension. I am thinking about a cat. So even if there are intensional entities, this is not what intentional objects are.

When something is a thing of a certain kind, there are general conditions that it meets which make it a thing of that kind. Here I do not want to propose any view about what these conditions might be in any detail; I'm just assuming that we do have an idea of such conditions, even if detailed accounts of them are disputable. For example, it is a necessary condition for something's being a physical object that it has a location in space-time. Or: it is a necessary condition of being a mental event that it exhibits either consciousness or intentionality or both. To develop a full account of mental and physical things or entities would be to elaborate what I shall call a 'substantial' conception of a thing or entity. A substantial conception of a thing tells us about the nature of that thing. Ontology deals in such substantial conceptions: an ontological theory of physical objects, for example, tells when such objects are the same or different, what the necessary conditions for being such an object are, and whether objects of these kinds are fundamental, or whether they reduce to other kinds of entity (that is, whether their existence and nature consists in the existence and nature of some other kind of thing).

What I am denying is that there is, or can be, any similarly substantial conception of intentional objects. This is the mistake of both unsatisfactory theories dismissed above: each theory assumes that they have to give an account of what intentional objects are, and then goes on to say either (with Searle) that the existence of intentional objects consists simply in the existence of some other 'ordinary' entities, or (with the theory of non-existent objects) that some intentional objects are non-existent entities. There is no necessary condition which something must meet in order to be an intentional object, in the sense of there being something substantial that all intentional objects in themselves have in common. There can be no substantial conception of intentional objects, since there is nothing entities have to be, in general and in themselves, in order to be intentional objects. Intentional objects, considered as such, have no nature.

Of course, it is true that all intentional objects are the objects of intentional states or acts. (By 'act' I mean a mental phenomenon that has an object and has a place in a time-series, like an act of judgement, or a decision.) But this doesn't mean that the *nature* of intentional objects is to be the objects of intentional states, in the sense that the nature of physical objects is to have a certain spatio-temporal location and to have certain physical properties. What is true, rather, is that something is an intentional object only in so far as it is an object *for* some thinker or some subject. 'Object' in this sense makes sense only relative to 'subject'. Objects are what is given or presented to subjects in intentional states of mind. When a real thing is given or presented to a subject there is nothing about it, considered in itself, which makes it the object of that subject's thought.

The fact that an intentional object is an object only *for* a subject entails the possibility that something might be an object for me, say, but not for you; or that certain kinds of minds or creatures can direct their minds on certain objects which are unavailable to other kinds. If you are more musically sophisticated than me, then you can hear things in music which I cannot; you may be able to hear an interrupted cadence in a piece of music which I cannot. The cadence is an object of your musical attention, but it is not an object of mine. It is an object *for you* but not an object *for me*. The high-pitched sounds which dogs can hear are objects for them but not for us; the colours of objects which sighted people see are objects for the sighted but not for the blind.

The idea of an intentional object, then, is similar to the idea of a *world*, in the sense in which a creature who is conscious can be said to 'have a world'. It is in this sense that the world of the blind is very different from the world of the sighted. 'World' in this sense is not, of course, the metaphysical idea of *all that is the case* or *the totality of facts*. I can say that the world of the blind is different from the world of the sighted without denying that there is one totality of facts. A.R. Luria's famous book, *The Man with the Shattered World* tells how the world is from the point of view of a soldier who has suffered massive brain damage, resulting in chaotic visual experience, impaired linguistic ability and little sense of himself as an integrated, unified locus of thought and consciousness.[11] The soldier's world is different from ours. It would be perverse to take this perfectly ordinary idiom to be purporting to imply that there is more than one world, in the sense of more than one totality of facts. Similarly, when I say that X is an intentional object for me but not for you (because you cannot, for some reason, apprehend X in an act of thought, say) I do not mean to imply that X *exists* in my world but not in yours, or that X *exists* for me, but not for you. X either exists or it does not. But whether or not it does has nothing to do with whether it is an intentional object for me or for you. Nonetheless, two people's thoughts can have the same intentional object, when they are thinking about (looking for, desiring, contemplating etc.) the same thing. To say that something is an object for me does not imply that it cannot be an object for you.

The idea of an object in this sense plays an important role in the theory of intentionality of Husserl and his followers. But in analytic philosophy, this kind of idea has been somewhat neglected. There are a number of different sources of this neglect. One is a deflationary tendency to treat the idea of an intentional object as a merely grammatical idea. This is the approach taken in a classic paper by Anscombe.[12] Anscombe claimed that to be an intentional object is to be a kind of *direct*

object in the grammatical sense, that is, the object of certain transitive verbs, which she calls intentional verbs. The comparison of
grammatical and intentional objects is illuminating; it shows
again how the word 'object', used in both cases in contrast with
'subject', does not always mean what it does in (e.g.) the phrase
'physical object'. A direct object is just what plays a certain role in
a sentence containing a transitive verb. However, we can find this
comparison illuminating without having to agree with Anscombe
that an intentional object is just the direct object of an intentional
verb; i.e. that the idea of an intentional object is really a grammatical idea. For one thing, Anscombe's criterion of what makes
a verb intentional is unsatisfactory, on at least two grounds. First,
it is really a criterion of intensionality, and as has often been
pointed out, that intensionality and intentionality are importantly
different concepts.[13] And second, Anscombe's criterion fails to
count 'belief' as an intentional verb (as she herself admits). But
surely an account of intentionality which does not put the
concept of belief at its centre is barely an account of intentionality at all.

In any case, it would surely be surprising if the idea of an intentional object, and related ideas like object of attention, object of
experience and object of thought, were mere shadows of the
grammar of our language (unless, of course, one held the implausible view that all philosophically interesting concepts were mere
shadows or artefacts of grammar). These ideas are phenomenological ideas, ideas we use in trying to articulate to ourselves the
fundamental nature of what our experience and thought is like.
Why should we expect the fundamental nature of experience and
thought to be *explained* in terms of grammar? If anything, the
explanation should be the other way around.

A more popular reason for the neglect of this idea of an intentional object in recent years is a certain re-alignment in discussions of intentionality. One dominant contemporary approach to
the problem of intentionality has identified intentionality with
representation. States of mind are representations: an *intentional
state* is one which involves a representation of things as being a
certain way. The state thus has a representational or intentional
content, which is how the world is represented as being. A desire
that *p*, a belief that *p*, an expectation or wish that *p*; all these
mental states have the same content, they involve a representa-

---

[13] See Searle 1983, ch. 1, and Crane 2001, §4.

tion of the world as being the *p*-way. In a desire, the world is desired to be the *p*-way, in a belief it is believed to be the *p*-way, and so on. The fundamental notions here are *representation, intentional state,* and *intentional* or *representational content.* One reason to avoid bringing in talk of intentional objects may be the one I located in my discussion of Searle's views above: all intentional states are about something (they have a content) but what they are about sometimes does not exist, so (given the equation of *object* and *entity*) their 'aboutness' in general cannot consist in a relation to an object/entity. So aboutness should just consist in a state's having an intentional or representational content. The concept of an intentional object is not one which a fully worked-out theory needs to employ.

I want to dispute this view, and argue for an indispensable role for the concept of an intentional object. In fact, I think that the concepts of intentional object and intentionality should be explained together with the concept of representation; intentionality cannot be explained in terms of representation. I say this not because I reject the idea of intentional content. On the contrary, I think we need both the idea of intentional object and the idea of intentional content in a proper account of intentionality.[14] Two states of mind may have the same intentional object – they may be about the same object – but differ in the way in which they present that object, or in what they predicate of it. These differences are differences in content. I would also claim that two intentional states may have the same content but differ in their objects (indexical thoughts are an example) but this use of 'content' is controversial and I won't defend it here. The content of a state of mind is, in a phrase of Valberg's, *what you would put into words*: when you put your thoughts into words, what you express is the content. (This is assuming, of course, that you have the words into which to put the thoughts. And this is also not to deny that there may be elements of content which cannot be put into words. It's just that what you *do* put into words, when you put your thought into words, is the content.) So I do not replace the talk of content with talk of objects; rather, I want to argue for an indispensable role for the idea of an intentional object. So we should not replace talk of intentionality and intentional objects with talk of representation or representational content. The two ways of talking should be understood together.

[14] For more details, see Crane 2001, §§5–8.

At first sight, one way in which it might seem as if the idea of representation is more straightforward than the idea of intentionality is that we are familiar with many everyday concrete examples of representations: written and spoken sentences, signs, pictures. Compared to these, the idea of something being an *object of thought* can seem worryingly insubstantial and evanescent. After all, here are the concrete things, the representations, before us: we can pick them up and manipulate them. Isn't this an indication that the idea of representation is a better starting point?

This is, of course, an illusion. Sentences and pictures are concrete representations; but no-one thinks that they represent in and of themselves. They have their power to represent only *derivatively*, deriving from the states of mind of thinkers who use them. To understand why these things are representations we need to appeal to the thoughts, intentions, plans and desires of thinkers: in short, their intentional states. Even those who follow Jerry Fodor, and think that these intentional states themselves involve sentences in a language of thought, do not think this because they think that sentences are in some way better equipped to represent the world, in and of themselves. No, the justification for the language of thought hypothesis derives from the systematic nature of mental processes, not from any assumption about the power of sentences to represent.[15] Those who defend the hypothesis are at pains to make it clear that postulating sentences in the head is one thing, and explaining how those sentences get their meaning – giving a 'semantics for the language of thought' – is quite another.

So familiar concrete representations get their meaning from the use that is made of them by thinkers. If we are to explain how the representational states of our minds 'get their meaning' then we had better do this in some other way. In what way? The standard approach among physicalist philosophers of mind is to give some account of what some call the 'representation relation' in non-intentional (usually causal) terms. But thus formulated, the project cannot succeed. For if it is possible to represent things which do not exist, then *there can be no representation relation*, since relations entail the existence of their relata. It follows from this that – whatever the other problems with the idea that representation reduces to causation – causation cannot underpin representation in general, since causation is a relation and representation

15 See, for example, Fodor 1987, Appendix.

isn't.[16] Beliefs might be relations to mental sentences; they might be relations to propositions; but none of this makes '*x* represents *y*' express a relation, if *x* can represent *y* when *y* does not exist.

These points might be acknowledged, but dismissed on the grounds that the causal model of representation being assumed is far too crude. This it doubtless is; the question is whether the more sophisticated versions of the theory can avoid this fundamental problem. The question is: where does one place the causal relation in a more sophisticated account? What role, precisely, does causation play? Could one say that causation can explain representation when the object represented does exist, but not when it doesn't? What, in that case, does one say about the case where the represented object does not exist? One proposal is that we should explain the representation in this case in terms of the represented item's *counterfactual* causal relation to the representation, rather than its *actual* causal relation.[17] Thus we might say, not that Pegasus causes my Pegasus-representations, but that Pegasus *would* cause my Pegasus-representations *were* he to exist; or alternatively, that what makes a representation a Pegasus-representation is that it *would* be caused by Pegasus in worlds in which he exists.

But even if this counterfactual is true, it is hard to see the proposal as an advance over the idea that one can represent things which do not exist. We started off with the idea that one could represent something even if that thing does not exist. Now this is supposed to be explained by the idea of a *causal relation that does not exist*. We are still in the position of needing an explanation of how something (either an object or a causal relation) which does not exist can be connected to an *actual* (not a counterfactual) thought about that 'something'. 'Representation' is certainly a good word for this connection, but in that case we should not think we have *explained* the representation of the non-existent in terms of a non-existent causal relation. How could this be an advance in our understanding?

It seems to me, then, that the appeal to causation in the theory of representation is a mere gesture unless it can say something more about the representation of the non-existent. Of course, it

---

[16] I assume here that causation is a relation, though this has been denied – for example by Mellor 1995.

[17] For a good account of the move from actual to counterfactual causal relations, see the introduction to Loewer and Rey, eds, 1993.

is true that thinkers think about many of the things they causally interact with, and that, in many cases, it is hard to see how they could have come to have thought about these things unless they had causally interacted with them. But what we are after, presumably, is not the causal history of this or that specific representation (or representation-type) but rather what makes representation possible in general. And no answer to this question is satisfactory unless it gives an answer to the question of representation of the non-existent.

So moving to the idea of representation has not enabled us to get away from the notion of what a representation is about; that is, its intentional object. For a representation is a representation of Pegasus not because it necessarily looks like Pegasus, nor because it is caused by Pegasus, but because it can be used to express thoughts (intentional states or acts) about Pegasus. A *mental* representation of Pegasus just is a thought (of some kind) about Pegasus. But to say that a thought is about Pegasus is to say that Pegasus is the intentional object of the thought. A thought's being about *x* and *x*'s being its intentional object are just the same idea. So as long as we talk about a thought's being about something, then we are talking in terms of intentional objects.

That we do employ the idea of a thought's being about something (and not just the idea of a thought's having representational content) is shown by the fact, noted above, that we can count thoughts as being about the same thing even when they have different contents. You might be thinking about Napoleon's exile on Elba, I might be thinking about his exile on St Helena. There is a sense in which we are thinking about the same thing: our thoughts have the same object. So we need more than the idea of content. This is hardly surprising: one of the intuitive glosses which we put on the notion of intentionality is that it is *aboutness*. And it is clearly a better starting-point to say that thoughts are about their objects than to say that they are about their contents. Thoughts *have* contents, and it is because of this that they are *about* their objects. Retaining the intuitive notion of aboutness means retaining the intuitive idea of what thoughts are about, and this in turn means retaining the idea of an intentional object.

In this paper, I have argued that the idea of an intentional object creates a dilemma for theories of intentionality: either intentional objects are ordinary existing entities, or they are the kind of entities some of which do not exist. If we say the first thing, then how do we make sense of intentional objects which do not exist? But if we say the second, then we have to accept the incredible view that there are non-existent entities. The way out of this dilemma is to deny an assumption made by each horn: that being an intentional object is being an entity of some sort. Rather, an intentional object is just the object (for some subject) of an intentional state or act. Of course, if all we have to say about intentional objects is that they are what intentional states are about, and all we have to say about intentional states is that they have objects, then the proposal is hopelessly circular. But a proper account of intentionality will have more to say, by giving a detailed account of the nature of various intentional phenomena. (I do not pretend to have even started on such an account here.) However, I believe, for the reasons given above, that a theory of intentionality will not be helped by appealing to causal relations between thoughts and their objects. And nor do I think that progress would be made by *replacing* talk of intentional objects with talk of representation. For a representation (linguistic, pictorial or mental) is the representation it is partly because of what it is about. And as long as we continue to make use of the idea of *what a mental state is about*, then we will need to make use of the idea of an intentional object.

Department of Philosophy
University College London
Gower Street
London WC1E 6BT
UK
Tim.crane@ucl.ac.uk

References

Anscombe, G.E.M. (1965). 'The Intentionality of Sensation: a grammatical feature', in R.J. Butler, ed., *Analytical Philosophy: 2ⁿᵈ Series*. Oxford: Blackwell, 158–80.
Crane, T. (2001). *Elements of Mind*. Oxford: Oxford University Press.
Fodor, J. (1987). *Psychosemantics*. Cambridge, Mass.: MIT Press.
Harman, G. (1990). 'The Intrinsic Quality of Experience', in J. Tomberlin, ed., *Philosophical Perspectives* 4. Atascadero, Ca.: Ridgeview. Reprinted in N. Block, O. Flanagan, and G. Güzeldere, eds, (1997) *The Nature of Consciousness*, Cambridge, Mass.: MIT Press, 663–676; page references to here.
Loewer, B. and G. Rey, eds, (1993). *Meaning in Mind*. Oxford: Blackwell.
Luria, A.R. (1987). *The Man with the Shattered World*. Cambridge, Mass.: Harvard University Press.
Martin, M.G.F. (1988). 'An Eye Directed Outward', in C. Wright, B.C. Smith, C. Macdonald, eds, *Knowing Our Own Minds*. Oxford: Oxford University Press, 99–122.
Mellor, D.H. (1995). *The Facts of Causation*. London: Routledge & Kegan Paul.

Parsons, T. (1980). *Non-existent Objects*. New Haven: Yale University Press.
Quine, W.V. (1953). 'On What There Is', in his *From a Logical Point of View*. Cambridge, Mass.: MIT Press, 1–19.
Searle, J. (1983). *Intentionality: an essay in the philosophy of mind*. Cambridge: Cambridge University Press.
Valberg, J.J. (1992). 'The Puzzle of Experience', in T. Crane, ed., *The Contents of Experience*. Cambridge: Cambridge University Press, 18–47.

CHAPTER 5

WHY COMPOSITIONALITY WON'T GO AWAY: REFLECTIONS ON HORWICH'S 'DEFLATIONARY' THEORY

Jerry Fodor and Ernie Lepore

Abstract
Paul Horwich argues for a 'deflationary' account of compositionality, according to which, '. . . the compositionality of meaning imposes no constraint at all on how the meaning properties of words are constituted'. We have arrived at a tentative diagnosis, which is that Horwich fails to enforce several distinctions that turn out to be crucial. For example, sometimes he puts his main conclusion in the way we just quoted but sometimes, even on the following page, he puts it like this: 'understanding one of one's own complex expressions (non-idiomatically) is, by definition, nothing over and above understanding its parts and knowing how they are combined'. We propose, in what follows, to consider how Horwich's deflationary account of compositionality fares if the distinction between theories of meaning and theories of understanding is properly attended to. Here's how we think it all turns out:

– Horwich is right to claim that compositionality is neutral with respect to the metaphysics of understanding expressions when 'understanding' refers to a (merely) dispositional state; but not when it refers to an occurrent state.
– Horwich is right *strictu dictu* to claim that compositionality is neutral with respect to the character of lexical meanings, but only *strictu dictu*.
– Compositionality taken, together with other constraints that semantic theories are required to satisfy, reduces the options in the theory of lexical meaning to a bare minimum.

The first part of the paper is about compositionality and understanding, the second part is about compositionality and lexical meaning.

Introduction

Compositionality is the idea that the meanings of complex expressions (or concepts) are constructed from the meanings of the less complex expressions (or concepts) that are their constituents.[1] Over the last few years, we have just about convinced ourselves that compositionality is the sovereign test for theories of lexical meaning.[2] So hard is this test to pass, we think, that it filters out practically all of the theories of lexical meaning that are current in either philosophy or cognitive science. Among the casualties are, for example, the theory that lexical meanings are statistical structures (like stereotypes); the theory that the meaning of a word is its use; the theory that knowing the meaning of (at least some) words requires having a recognitional capacity for (at least some) of the things that it applies to; and the theory that knowing the meaning of a word requires knowing criteria for applying it. Indeed, we think that only two theories of the lexicon survive the compositionality constraint: *viz.*, the theory that all lexical meanings are primitive and the theory that some lexical meanings are primitive and the rest are definitions. So compositionality does a lot of work in lexical semantics, according to our lights.

Well, so imagine our consternation and surprise when, having just about convinced ourselves of all this, we heard that Paul Horwich has on offer a 'deflationary' account of compositionality, according to which, '. . . the compositionality of meaning imposes *no constraint at all* on how the meaning properties of words are constituted' (p. 154; our emphasis).[3] Surely, we thought, that can't be right; surely compositionality must rule out at least *some* theories about what word meanings are; for example, the theory that they are rocks, or that they are sparrows or chairs; for how could the meanings of complex expressions be constructed from any of those? What, we wondered, is going on here?

We have arrived at a tentative diagnosis, which is that Horwich fails to enforce several distinctions that turn out to be crucial. For example, sometimes he puts his main conclusion in the way we quoted above: 'the compositionality of meaning imposes no constraint at all on how the meaning properties of words are constituted'. But sometimes, even on the following

---

[1] We assume, for the present discussion, that words express concepts, and that the content of a word is the content of the concept that it expresses. So we'll move back and forth from talk of words to talk of concepts as convenience of exposition suggests. This is, to be sure, to simplify some complicated matters. But it doesn't affect any of the questions that we disagree with Horwich about.

[2] See Fodor and Lepore 1991; Fodor and Lepore 1996; and papers in Fodor 1998.

[3] All references are to Horwich 1998, unless otherwise stated.

page, he puts it like this: 'understanding one of one's own complex expressions (non-idiomatically) is, by definition, nothing over and above understanding its parts and knowing how they are combined' (p. 155). Now, *prima facie*, these wouldn't seem to be at all the same theses. Whereas the first purports to answer a question about the metaphysics of *meaning, viz.*, 'What linguistic facts about a complex expression are the supervenience base for its meaning properties?',[4] the second purports to answer a question about the metaphysics of *understanding, viz.*, 'What makes it true of a speaker that he understands an expression in his language?'.[5]

We propose, in what follows, to consider how Horwich's deflationary account of compositionality fares if the distinction between theories of meaning and theories of understanding is properly attended to. Here's how we think it all turns out:

– Horwich is right to claim that compositionality is neutral with respect to the metaphysics of understanding expressions when 'understanding' refers to a (merely) dispositional state; *but not when it refers to an occurrent state.*
– Horwich is right *strictu dictu* to claim that compositionality is neutral with respect to the character of lexical meanings, but only *strictu dictu.*
– Compositionality taken *together with other constraints that semantic theories are required to satisfy* reduces the options in the theory of lexical meaning to the bare minimum enumerated above.

The first part of the paper is about compositionality and understanding, the second part is about compositionality and lexical meaning.

---

[4] It adds to the confusion that although philosophers sometimes use 'how are word meanings constituted?' to ask what word meanings are, they sometimes use it to ask a quite different question, *viz.*, what is it about an expression in virtue of which it means what it does? This last question comes up in, e.g., discussions of the 'naturalization' of semantics. Possible answers include: 'it's causal relations'; 'it's something teleological'; 'it's the communicative intentions of speaker/hearers, or the tacit conventions that they adhere to'; etc. We mention this only by way of clearing the air. It's not what either we or Horwich have in mind in the present discussion.

[5] There are philosophers who hold, as a matter of doctrine, that nothing could be a theory of meaning that isn't also a theory of understanding. Thus Michael Dummett: 'Any theory of meaning which was not, or did not immediately yield, a theory of understanding, would not satisfy the purpose for which, philosophically, we require a theory of meaning.' (Dummett 1993, p. 4). Perhaps Horwich accepts this view; he doesn't say.

Part I: Compositionality and Understanding

Here's one version of what Horwich calls 'the basic thesis' of his paper: '. . . once one has worked out how a certain sentence is constructed from primitive syntactic elements, and provided one knows the meanings of those elements, then, automatically and without further ado, one qualifies as understanding the sentence' (p. 155). We will presently argue that the question whether working out its syntax and its lexical content suffices for understanding a sentence is quite independent of the question whether compositionality constrains theories of lexical meaning. But, for the moment, we proceed to consider Horwich's account of understanding in its own right.

We think there is a (perhaps slightly forced) sense in which grasping its syntax and lexicon is indeed sufficient for understand the meaning of a sentence or other complex expression. But we also think that there's another sense in which it's pretty clearly not. For compositionality implies that, if you are given the syntax and the lexical content of an expression, you have all the information that's relevant to what it means, hence everything you need to understand it. (Maybe there are still things that you need to know about the world; e.g., what in the world the demonstratives demonstrate. But this isn't the sort of issue that either we or Horwich are concerned with.) And we think that there is a sense of 'understanding an expression' in which having all the information that's relevant to understanding it *is* understanding it. This is the notion of understanding that is in play when, for example, linguists say that, *qua* English speaker, you here and now understand infinitely many English sentences, including infinitely many whose tokens you have never encountered and never will.

However, there is also a perfectly natural sense of understanding an expression in which you can *fail* to understand one when you encounter it, *even though* you know the language that it belongs to. It's in this sense of 'understanding an expression' that one may still have some figuring out to do even after having grasped the linguistic properties on which the meaning of the expression supervenes. To see that such a situation can arise, consider sentence S, about whose syntax and lexical inventory we will now tell you the complete and unvarnished truth:

S: 'Dogs dogs dogs dog dog dogs.'

Lexicon:

'dog$_N$' means dog
'-s' means plural
'dog$_V$' means to dog

Syntax:

[[Dogs$_N$ [dogs$_{N1}$ [dogs$_{N2}$ dog$_{V2}$]$_{NP}$]$_{NP}$]]$_{NP}$ [dog$_{V1}$ [dogs$_{N3}$]]$_{VP}$]$_S$

Clearly, someone might know everything we've just specified about its lexicon and syntax and nevertheless not understand S. Horwich discusses this sort of case, but only very, very briefly. He says, 'clearly the length and complexity of expressions whose structures we are able to discern are constrained by psychological factors' (p. 167). These, however, are constraints on our 'ability to understand . . . words and appreciate how they are combined; but the compositionality of meaning is not amongst those conditions.' As far as we can make out, the idea here is that it's stuff *about our psychology* that explains our problems with S, *therefore it is not* facts about S's compositional structure. But if that is the intended argument, the premise clearly doesn't warrant the conclusion. Consider the following Silly Argument:

Silly Argument: It's stuff about your muscles that explains why you can't lift this rock, *therefore it's not* stuff about what the rock weighs.

Surely, the right answer to the Silly Argument is that it's *both* stuff about your muscles *and* stuff about what the rock weighs that explains why you can't lift it. It's *because* the rock weighs what it does that you can't lift it with the muscles you've got. Well, likewise: if you continue to have trouble with S even after we've told you its syntax and lexical inventory, that's surely because there are psychological limits that make it hard to appreciate how the syntax and lexical inventory combine to determine its meaning. To put it another way, if one continues to have trouble understanding S, that's because *an inference is required* to get from a grasp of the lexical/syntactic facts on which its meaning *supervenes* to understanding what its meaning *is*. This is tantamount to endorsing Horwich's 'objection 8', which goes as follows: 'The deflationary account fails to do justice to the intuition that we *figure out* the meanings of complex expressions on the basis of our knowledge of what their parts mean . . . [it's] not just that the *facts* about the meanings of primitives determine the *facts* about the meanings of the complexes. It's rather that our *knowledge* of the basic facts must lead by some inferential process to our *knowledge* of what the complexes mean' (p. 171; italics are in the original). To which objection Horwich replies: 'this is indeed a tempting intuition; but [the thesis that understanding complex expressions requires inferences] cannot be correct, and so the deflationary attitude should not be faulted for failing to respect it' (p. 171). We'll come in a moment to *why* Horwich says this tempting intuition 'cannot be correct'. For the moment, we want to go on a bit about just how tempting the intuition is. An analogy should help. Consider claims (i) and (ii) about checking accounts:

i. If you know what your balance was when you started, and what you have deposited, and what you have drawn out, then you know what the balance of your account is.

ii. If you know the things (i) enumerates, you needn't do anything more (in particular, you needn't do anything inferential) to figure out what your balance is.

We take it that (i) is approximately truistic; it follows from *what sort of thing a balance is* (or, if you prefer, it follows from what 'balance' means).[6] Our point, anyhow, is that (ii) doesn't follow from (i) and, moreover, that (ii) is implausible on the face of it.

Why (ii) doesn't follow from (i).

The following schema has the form of an intentional fallacy:

iii. That it is the case that P determines (nomically, metaphysically, or conceptually) that it is the case that Q.
iv. Jones knows that it's the case that P.
v. Therefore: Jones knows that it's the case that Q.

Accordingly, the following substitution instance of the schema is invalid:

vi. That one started with three dollars in the account, deposited two dollars and withdrew one dollar determines that the current balance is four dollars.
vii. Jones knows that he started with three dollars in the account . . . etc.

[6] We don't like the parenthesized way of talking; we like to keep our metaphysics clear of our semantics. But the present issues don't in any way turn on that, so we're prepared to be concessive.

viii. Therefore: Jones knows that his current balance is four dollars.

We suppose that (ix)–(xi) is likewise invalid and for the same reasons.

ix. That 'John' means *John*, 'loves' means *loves* and 'Mary' means *Mary* (together with syntax) determines that 'John loves Mary' means *John loves Mary*.

x. Bill knows that 'John' means *John*, and that 'Mary' means *Mary*, etc.

xi. Therefore: Bill knows that 'John loves Mary' means *John loves Mary*.

We can now see just why, though there is 'a sense in which' it's sufficient for understanding a complex expression that one grasps its syntax and the meaning of its constituents, there is also 'a sense in which' it isn't. What usually happens when P is metaphysically sufficient for Q is that the inference *believes (. . .P. . .)* → *believes (. . .Q. . .)* is valid on one way of reading 'believes' but invalid on another.

Let's see where things stand. We're pretty sure that Horwich would agree with the intuition that there's a robust reading of 'know one's balance' on which the inference (vi)–(viii) is fallacious. But we take it that he denies the putative analogy to (ix)–(xi). Why? Well because, in the linguistic case, 'transitions between states of understanding do not work in this way, because the beliefs involved in knowledge of meanings are *implicit* [*sic*] . . . But since [those beliefs are] implicit, *[and thus consist] in no more than the fact that the expression means a certain thing in his idiolect*, its explanation should not be expected to involve inferential processes' (pp. 171–172, our emphasis).

So the difference between the checkbook case, where we take it that Horwich accepts the 'tempting intuition' that there is figuring out going on, and the language understanding case, where he rejects it, is that whereas the beliefs germane to checkbook balancing are explicit, the beliefs germane to sentence understanding are not. This difference matters, according to Horwich, because of a certain metaphysical truth about tacit knowledge: *Qua ex*plicit, your current belief that you have four dollars in the bank is constituted by your being in a mental state with certain causal powers; presumably the sorts of causal powers that affect 'transitions between states of understanding' and that are manifested when you think, talk, etc. about what you have in the bank. But, *qua implicit*,[7] your tacit belief that 'John runs' means *John runs* is constituted simply by the fact that you take 'John' to mean *John* and 'runs' to mean *runs* (and the syntax to be what it is). So, on this account, there's a deep difference between the metaphysics of tacit belief and the metaphysics of explicit belief.

Now, to be perfectly frank, we find this all very dark. It is, in particular, quite unclear to us why implicit beliefs should be supposed to differ, in any such way, from explicit ones. For all we know, and, certainly, for all that Horwich has argued, *implicitly* believing that *S means P* and *explicitly* believing that *S means P* might both turn out to be having your brain in a certain functional or neurological state; or they might both turn out to be having a Mentalese sentence that means that *S means P* tokened in your belief box. . .; or whatever. If any such story is right, then it's not clear why the two kinds of beliefs mightn't be acquired by much the same kinds of inferential processes.

We can now say more clearly what our argument with Horwich is about. We think he is right that there is a kind of case (quite different from checkbook balancing) in which all that's required for grasping something complex is having the right beliefs about its structure and constituents. We take it that Horwich agrees there is a kind of case (of which checkbook balancing is an example) where having the right beliefs about its structure and constituents is *not* sufficient for grasping something complex. However, Horwich thinks the difference between the two kinds of cases is that, in the first but not the second, the beliefs about the constituents of the expression are *implicit*. By contrast, we think the difference is that, in the second but not the first, the understanding of the complex is (merely) *dispositional* (where the contradictory of (merely) *dispositional* is something like *occurrent*).

Notice that, though both apply (*inter alia*) to mental states, implicit/explicit is a quite different kind of distinction from occurrent/dispositional. The former is epistemological; it's a matter of whether the creature that's in a state has (non-inferential) access to its being there. In the simplest examples,

---

[7] Or perhaps it's *qua* implicit knowledge of one's own idiolect (see Horwich's fn. 14, p. 172). We're not clear whether Horwich holds a deflationary view of implicit knowledge *per se*, or just about implicit knowledge of language. Nothing, however, turns on this in the arguments that follow.

implicit/explicit is about whether a creature is able to report being in the state that it's in. Whereas the second distinction is *ontological;* we suppose that *occurrents,* but not dispositions, are species of events. That is part and parcel of the fact that they are associated not just with *stretches* of time, but also with *instants.* If John's thought that the cat is trapped in the closet is occurrent, then 'when did it occur to him?' presumably has an answer ('at 3:17'; 'when he first heard the cat say meow' and so forth.) But if his thought that the cat is trapped in the closet is merely dispositional (as in the case where John is congenitally disposed to occurrent *cat-in-the-closet* thoughts) the pertinent question is not 'when did it occur to him?' but 'how long did it last?' ('How lonk haf you been vorryink about die gats' beink in de gloset, Mister Portnoy?') We're aware, of course, that it's in dispute just how the distinction between dispositions and occurrents should be drawn, and we don't want to get involved in the argument. Suffice it that it's metaphysical rather than epistemic by general consensus; hence, by general consensus, different from implicit/explicit.

So, then, our story is that one's understanding of a sentence can be any combination of explicit/implicit with occurrent/dispositional (except that an explicit mental state presumably has to be occurrent; see fn. 7) In the case where one's understanding of an expression is implicit and (merely) dispositional, Horwich may well be right that it comes to no more than one's grasp of the syntax and the meanings of the parts. However, we think that's because such cases are *dispositional,* not because they're *implicit.* That is, like all our cognitive scientist friends, we think there is such a thing as understanding that is implicit but *occurrent* (a species of unconscious mental process, we suppose). Certainly Horwich hasn't given any reason to doubt that there's such a thing. Nor has he given any reason to believe that, when implicitly understanding a sentence is an occurrent process, inferring the sentence's compositional structure from its lexical and syntactic structure is other than essential.

We're pretty sure we have this stick by the right end since we can't think of any reason why an occurrent belief shouldn't be arrived at inferentially, whether or not it's explicit. By contrast a (merely) dispositional belief can't be arrived at *inferentially* because it can't be *arrived at* at all. There might, of course, be mental processes that cause you to have a (merely) dispositional belief; and some of the episodes in such mental processes might consist of having thoughts occur to you. But these thoughts wouldn't count as premises from which the dispositional belief is *inferred.* You can't *infer* that P unless it (implicitly or explicitly) *occurs to you* that P; and (merely) dispositional beliefs are *ipso facto not* ones that (implicitly or explicitly) occur to you.

Here's where we've got to now. It's urged against the deflationary account of compositionality that it 'fails to do justice to the intuition that we *figure out* the meanings of complex expressions on the basis of our *knowledge* of what their parts mean . . .'. Not so, Horwich replies; though it's tempting to think that understanding complex expressions depends on inferences from their syntactic and lexical constituency, that thought must be resisted when the beliefs involved are implicit. Horwich offers no argument for this, however, and he needs one badly. For, the obvious candidates for non-inferential beliefs about the meanings of complex expressions aren't the *implicit* ones, they're the (merely) *dispositional* ones. If that's right, then there is no reason so far why some of one's beliefs about expressions shouldn't be both implicit and occurrent. And there is no reason so far why these *implicit,* occurrent beliefs about expressions shouldn't be much like one's *explicit,* occurrent beliefs about one's balance; *viz.,* both inferential. We suspect, in short, that Horwich has confused the distinction between implicit and explicit beliefs with the distinction between (merely) dispositional and occurrent beliefs, and that this has led him to argue, in effect, that since when beliefs about expressions are dispositional they aren't inferential, it follows that when they are implicit they also aren't inferential. But this argument turns on a conflation.[8]

However, we're still not out of the woods. For, according to Horwich there is an independent argument against the 'tempting intuition' that sentence understanding, like checkbook balancing, can involve a lot of 'figuring out', i.e., an argument that *doesn't* assume that implicit knowledge is *ipso facto* non-inferential, but that shows all the same that '. . . at the fundamental level, compositionality is not explained in terms of inference' (p. 174). Here's the argument: '. . . although there may be *some* language whose complex expressions are understood as a product of explicit inference, such inferences would have to take place in a more

---

[8] Notice that whereas (according to us) implicit beliefs may nonetheless be occurrent, it's presumably a truism that explicit beliefs can't be merely dispositional. Perhaps it's because the two distinctions fail, in this respect, to be independent that Horwich got confused between them.

basic language whose complexes would themselves already have to have some content or meaning; and if inferences are required for this, then a yet more basic language would be needed in which to conduct them . . . and so on' (p. 172).[9]

This regress argument has been around for a long time; probably it was invented by someone who lived in a cave. The usual reply strikes us as convincing: by assumption, understanding English expressions is inferential because you have to translate English sentences into some other language (into Mentalese as it might be) in order to use the information they convey. But you don't have to translate Mentalese into some other language in order to use the information its expressions convey. All you have to do is think in it. So there isn't a regress after all.

But Horwich isn't having that. 'It is all very well to refuse to speak of "understanding" and "possession" of meaning in connection with the language of thought, and thereby to hope to retain the idea that when a complex is, properly speaking, "understood", inference is invariably involved . . . [But that] merely obscures the fact that the same issues [about compositionality] arise with respect to Mentalese, but in a slightly different formulation' (p. 173).

Let's, please, be very careful about what's at issue here. To begin with, we're quite prepared to concede, for purposes of the argument, that someone who thinks in Mentalese thereby counts as understanding it 'in some sense'. *Pace* Horwich, what we've called 'the usual reply' to the regress argument is not supposed to be terminological. In particular, it's not supposed to turn on whether what one does with Mentalese counts, *strictu dictu*, as understanding it. Rather, the issue is whether assuming that English and Mentalese are both compositional and that understanding English is inferential, requires assuming that whatever constitutes understanding Mentalese is inferential too. Horwich apparently thinks we must; we think we needn't, and we affirm that we don't.

The following view seems to us coherent and neither vacuous nor gratuitous: English is compositional, and the process of understanding its sentences is inferential. But the fact that the process of understanding English sentences is *inferential doesn't*

---

[9] There's something puzzling about this formulation. Presumably, it's a mistake for Horwich to suggest that the inferences that generate the regress have to be *explicit*. If a regress threatens, it's because of the putative necessary connection between understanding a language and making *any inferences at all*, explicit or otherwise. We'll take this reading for granted in what follows.

follow from the fact that English is compositional. So far, then, there's nothing to prevent a language from being compositional even though the process of understanding its sentences *isn't* inferential. If this possibility is coherent and begs no questions, then assuming that understanding English is inferential, *and* that all inference requires a linguistic vehicle, *and* that one thinks in sentences of Mentalese implies no regress so far.

Can one conjure up a plausible story according to which all of that is true? Sure; in fact, it's just the standard language of thought story. Readers who have already heard this story, and are tired of it, are advised to skip directly to Part 2.

We need, in particular, two assumptions:

xii. The mental processes that are the consequences of understanding a sentence are mediated by a mental representation which displays its logical form; this is true both of English and of Mentalese.

xiii. Sentences of Mentalese are explicit about their logical form (in ways which, notoriously, those of English are not).

If (xii) and (xiii) are both true, then inference might enter into one's use of English in a way that it doesn't enter into one's use of Mentalese, even though Mentalese and English are both compositional. That's because, in the case of Mentalese but not in the case of English, the truth of (xiii) assures that (xii) is satisfied vacuously. The trick, to repeat, is to motivate the claim that understanding English is inferential *independently* of motivating the claim that it is compositional, thus leaving open the possibility that Mentalese might be compositional even though inference isn't required to use it. As far as we can tell, Horwich offers no argument at all against this tactic; it appears, indeed, that he is unaware of its existence as a polemical possibility.

Notice that we don't have to show that there is such a language in order to undermine Horwich's regress argument; all that's required is that (xii) and (xiii) are coherent. Still, as a matter of fact, our main reason for thinking they are coherent is that we think they are probably both true. So we'll say a little about that.

– *Why you might want to endorse what (xii) says about English.*

Because you think that understanding an English sentence involves representing it in a way that formally determines its entailments, and that logical form does so but surface structure doesn't.

Because you think that understanding an English sentence requires (*inter alia*) recovering an ambiguity-free representation of the sentence; *a fortiori*, it requires recovering a representation which distinguishes ambiguities of logical syntax.

Because you hold a computational view of mental processes according to which the consequences of understanding an English sentence are determined by mental operations that are sensitive to the logical form of the sentence.

There are other reasons too. But these should do to be getting on with.

– Why you might want to endorse what (xii) says about Mentalese.

Because you hold a view of mental processes according to which the psychological consequences of tokening a Mentalese sentence are causally determined by operations that (a) are responsive to its logical form and (b) apply to the sentence in virtue of its syntax. Making the logical form of a Mentalese sentence explicit in its syntax is how to meet both these conditions at once. As, indeed, Turing taught us.

– Why you might want to endorse (xiii).

Precisely in order to avoid the regress that threatens if you have to *infer* the logical syntax of a Mentalese sentence in order for it to play its characteristic causal role. Roughly, if (xiii) is true, then all that is required for it to play this role is that it be tokened (e.g., in the belief box.) That's *why* talk of understanding a Mentalese sentence is otiose in a way that talk of understanding an English sentence is not.

So then: We hold that no regress threatens the view that English and Mentalese are both compositional and that understanding English requires a kind of inference and that thinking in Mentalese does not.

Suppose, however, that we're wrong about all this and there is, after all, some way to show that language understanding isn't inferential. What would that imply about the deflation of compositionality? In particular, what would it imply about whether the compositionality of a language constrains the semantics of its lexicon? We think the right answer is 'Nothing'.

The patient reader will remember that Horwich has two formulations of his 'main thesis', these being that 'compositionality of meaning imposes no constraint at all on how the meaning properties of words are constituted' and that 'understanding a complex expression (non-idiomatically) is, by definition, nothing over and above understanding its parts and knowing how they are combined'. We now return to a point that we made at the outset: Though Horwich asserts them interchangeably, these two formulations don't appear to be equivalent; in particular, the second doesn't appear to imply the first. Correspondingly, if it's the first that one really cares about, it doesn't matter whether the second is true. So then, after all this ground clearing, we propose to put the issues about how (/whether) understanding sentences requires making inferences entirely to one side. That allows us to turn directly to the question: 'does an account of the compositionality of a language constrain the nature of its lexicon?' We'll now argue that *of course it does.*

Part II: Compositionality and the Lexicon

We started this paper by rehearsing a familiar informal construal of the notion of compositionality: in effect, that the meanings of complex expressions supervene on their syntax together with the meanings of the lexical primitives they contain. We remarked that if a language is compositional in that sense, then, *prima facie,* that imposes some quite significant constraints on what the meanings of its primitives could be. It's hard to see, for example, how primitive meanings could be birds or chairs since, whatever complex meanings may be, it's hard to see how birds or chairs could be parts of them.

You might suppose that Horwich would find this line of thought anathema; but he needn't, and as far as we can tell he doesn't. For, our way of putting the point assumes that the meanings of complex expressions *contain* the meanings of primitive expressions (so that the meaning of 'loves' is part of the meaning of 'John loves Mary' and so on). Such assumptions are not, however, entailed by the supervenience thesis *per se.* Supervenience *per se* entails only that *whatever the semantic facts about complex expressions may turn out to be,* they are determined by their syntax together with the semantic facts about their lexical primitives, whatever *they* may turn out to be.

Horwich's deflationary story about compositionality is only this: compositionality places no constraint on primitive meanings *if one prescinds* from all assumptions about *complex* meanings except that they supervene on syntax and lexical inventory. For, as Horwich says, '. . . *whatever* their underlying nature may turn out to be, there are bound to be construction properties (of the form 'x [= the meaning of the complex] results from applying procedure p to primitives whose meanings are, $<W_1, . . ., W_n>$)'. Hence . . . it is bound to be the case that the facts regarding the meanings of the complex expressions are derived from facts about the meanings of the primitives' (p. 160, our emphasis). We take this to be just the point that, *if it's left open* what the semantic facts about the complexes are, then, whatever the meanings of the primitives are, there is sure to be some way of mapping the latter onto the former. If *that's* all that semantic compositionality requires, then, as Horwich says, it can't but be true.

But all that shows is that the unexiguous notion of compositionality that follows from supervenience alone isn't the robust notion of compositionality that a theory of sentence meaning requires. And, if that's all that the deflation of compositionality amounts to, it's of no great interest that compositionality deflates. People who think that compositionality substantively constrains lexical meaning have it in mind that there are all sorts of presumptive truths about the semantics of complex expressions that need explaining; and that it's precisely the assumption of compositionality, together with a theory of the primitive meanings, that is supposed to explain them. Such presumptive truths about complex meanings as these, for example:

– Complex meanings are semantically evaluable (e.g., for truth or satisfaction).
– Although the syntax and lexicon of English are finitely specifiable, there is a denumerable infinity of distinct complex meanings.
– There are n-complex meanings for each intuitively n-ways ambiguous complex English expression.
– One meaning of the sentence 'John ate his peas' is such that 'John' has scope over 'his'.
– The meaning of 'John snores' and the meaning of 'John swims' are such that both sentences make reference to John.

And so on and on. And on.

Consider, for a further example, the arguments about systematicity that are currently live in cognitive science. Roughly, systematicity is the fact that any language (/mind) that can express (/entertain) the proposition P will also be able to express (/entertain) many propositions that are semantically close to P: Anyone who can think the thoughts that *John snores* and that *flounders swim* can likewise think the thoughts that *flounders snore* and that *John swims*. (Likewise, *mutatis mutandis*, for understanding sentences of a language that can express these thoughts.)

It's pretty widely agreed that an explanation of the fact that complex meanings are systematic requires assuming that lexical meanings are context independent. The idea is this: compositionality says that the meaning of 'John snores' and of 'John swims' depend, *inter alia*, on the meaning of 'John'. And it's because 'John' means the same in the context '. . .snores' as it does in the context '. . .swims' that if you know what 'John' means in one context you thereby know what it means in the other.

So compositionality, together with the systematicity of complex meanings, places a context-independence constraint on the properties of lexical meanings. This constraint is *highly substantive*. For example, it rules out the theory, held practically universally in the cognitive psychology community, that concepts are stereotypes. The argument goes like this: the systematicity of complex meanings requires the context-independence of lexical meanings; stereotypes aren't context independent (for example, the stereotype of people-swimming is much different from the stereotype of flounder-swimming since the latter, but not the former, adverts to the exercise of fins); so lexical meanings can't be stereotypes.

This seems a pretty good example of how compositionality, together with other considerations about complex expressions, constrains the semantics of primitive expressions. Horwich, considering this case, replies that the argument from compositionality to concepts, lexical meanings, etc., not being stereotypes presupposes a 'uniformity thesis'; *viz.*, that if the meanings of the primitives are stereotypes (or uses, or prototypes, or inferential roles, or whatever), then the meanings of the complexes are *also* stereotypes (uses, prototypes, inferential roles, etc.). Well, it doesn't, since, as we've just seen, a context-independence thesis would do equally well; and context-independence is a property that compositionality imposes on the lexicon *whether or not* uniformity is assumed.

Anyhow, there is an independent argument for the uniformity principle. Compositionality says, roughly, that its syntax and its lexical constituents determine the meaning of a complex expression; it's thus part of the explanation of why practically everybody who understands 'dogs' and 'bark' understands 'dogs bark.' But it also needs explaining that you practically never find people who understand 'dogs bark' but don't understand 'dogs' or 'bark'. What we'll call *'reverse'* compositionality explains this by assuming that each constituent expression contributes *the whole of* it's meaning to its complex hosts. If that's right, then if you understand 'dogs bark,' it follows that you know everything you need to determine the meanings of 'dog' and 'bark': in effect, the meanings of the parts of a complex expression supervene on the meaning of that expression.

Now, as far as anybody knows, compositionality and reverse compositionality *always go together.* Just as you won't find a language that can talk about dogs and barking but can't talk about dogs barking, so you won't find a language that can talk about dogs barking but can't say anything else about barking or about dogs. It would be nice to have an explanation of why the meanings of complex expressions supervene on the meanings of their parts; and of why the meanings of parts supervene on the meanings of their complex hosts. And it would be still nicer if the explanation of these two superveniences also explained why they always turn up together. In fact, the explanation is obvious; the meaning of 'dogs bark' supervenes on the meanings of 'dogs' and 'bark' because the meanings of 'dogs' and 'bark' are parts of the meaning of 'dogs bark'; and *the meanings of 'dogs' and 'bark' supervene on the meaning of 'dogs bark' for exactly the same reason.* But the idea that complex meanings (don't just supervene on, but actually contain) the constituent meanings, is the 'uniformity thesis' in a very strong form. So it looks like the uniformity thesis must be true. So it looks like compositionality (together with reverse compositionality, together with the lack of an alternative explanation) severely constrains the lexicon after all; for example, it entails that lexical meanings can't be stereotypes.

This sort of argument ramifies in interesting ways. The meanings of 'dogs' and 'bark' must be contained in the meaning of 'dogs bark' because people who understand the sentence likewise understand the words. But the meaning of 'dogs bark' must be contained in the meaning of 'dogs bark and cats purr' because people who understand the conjunctive sentence generally understand both conjuncts.[10] In fact, the reverse compositionality of complex expressions relative to their *lexical* constituents, is just

---

[10] It's not, of course, a *necessary* truth that if you understand a syntactically conjunctive sentence you understand each syntactic conjunct; the sentence might be an idiom.

a special case of the reverse compositionality of complex expressions with respect to their constituents *tout court*, lexical or otherwise. Since, in natural languages, every constituent expression has infinitely many hosts, this amounts to an infinite amount of reverse compositionality, all of which is, as far as anybody knows, inexplicable unless the 'uniformity condition' is assumed. (For further discussion of the implications of reverse compositionality see Fodor, 1998, chs. 4, 5.)

The point we want to emphasize, however, is not that the reverse compositionality argument against stereotypes as lexical meanings is correct (though it is). Our point is that people who think it matters to the lexicon whether complex meanings are compositional have it in mind to deploy arguments that include many premises about the semantics of complex expressions over and above the assumption that sentence meanings are compositional: that sentence meanings are systematic, that languages and conceptual systems are reverse compositional, that complex meanings are uniform with lexical meanings, etc. It's quite true, as Horwich says, that compositionality doesn't matter much lacking further such assumptions. But it's also true that it doesn't matter much that compositionality doesn't matter much lacking such further assumptions. What matters is that there appears to be a plethora of truths about the semantics of complex expressions that the assumption of compositionality, together with a good theory of the lexicon, explains; and that, as far as anybody knows, can't be explained if the assumption of compositionality is left out.

Summary and Conclusion

This was the burden of Part 1: The standard reasons for holding that understanding English sentences requires making inferences are all basically 'poverty of the stimulus' arguments. They depend on claiming, on one hand, that the surface structure of English sentences is generally inexplicit about semantically salient properties of logical form; and, on the other hand, that properties of the logical forms of sentences are essential determinants of the causal consequences of their tokenings. That is all quite compatible with supposing that, although Mentalese is compositional, you don't have to understand it in order to think in it.

This was the burden of Part 2: The standard arguments that run from compositionality to the nature of lexical meaning turn on the need to explain such familiar properties of complex meanings as productivity, systematicity, reverse compositionality and the like. It is therefore not surprising, and not awfully interesting, that compositionality is deflatable when one abstracts from its role in such explanations. Why, after all, should anyone *want* to abstract from the role of compositionality in explaining systematicity, productivity and the like? Natural languages, and human minds, *are* systematic and productive, and that they are needs explaining.

Anyhow, as far as we can tell, the argument discussed in Part 1 that understanding English requires making inferences, and the argument discussed in Part 2 that compositionality constrains lexical semantics, are independent in both directions. Thus, the compositionality argument that shows that lexical meanings can't be stereotypes applies both to English and Mentalese, even though, by assumption, using the former requires making inferences but using the latter doesn't. Conversely, there presumably could be a language whose use has to be inferential (e.g., because its formulas aren't explicit about their logical forms) but which is none the less not compositional. A finite language, all of whose expressions are idioms, would do the trick.[11] The long and short is: All that the claim that understanding English requires inference and the claim that compositionality constrains lexical semantics have in common is that there are convincing arguments for each of them.

Centre for Cognitive Science
Rutgers University
Piscataway, NJ 08854-8020
lepore@ruccs.rutgers.edu

References

Dummett, M. (1993). *The Seas of Language.* Oxford: Oxford University Press.
Fodor, J. (1998). *In Critical Condition.* Cambridge, Mass.: MIT Press.
Fodor, J. and E. Lepore (1991). 'Why Meaning (Probably) Isn't Conceptual Role'. *Mind and Language* 6, 329–43.
Fodor, J. and E. Lepore (1996). 'The Pet Fish and the Red Herring; Why Concepts Aren't Prototypes'. *Cognition* 58, 243–276.
Horwich, P. (1998). *Meaning.* Oxford: Oxford University Press.

[11] Because he holds that compositionality places no substantive constraints theories of language, Horwich is presumably required to hold that being compositional is not a property that languages have *contingently*. (See his discussion of objection 5.) It would seem to follow that the meanings of complex expressions must supervene on their syntax and lexical contents *even in a finite language*. This strikes us as a *reductio;* surely a finite language could consist only of idioms?

CHAPTER 6

DEFLATING COMPOSITIONALITY

Paul Horwich

Abstract
My approach to the compositionality of meaning is deflationary in two respects. In the first place it shows that there is no need for a Tarski-style truth-theoretic account of it, and thereby avoids the difficult methodological and technical problems that would have to be solved on such an account. And in the second place it shows that compositionality imposes no constraint whatsoever on theories of lexical meaning. On the first of these points I am opposing Davidson and the tradition in semantics that he instigated. On the second point I am opposing Fodor and Lepore who have denounced various accounts of lexical meaning (including the one I favour – the use theory) for not squaring with compositionality. My plan for this paper is to outline the deflationary approach, to sketch its advantages, and to defend it against objections that have been made by Davidson, Fodor and Lepore.

What kind of assumptions about a foreign speaker would put us in a position to interpret each of the unlimited number of things he might say, and how could such assumptions be verified? Like Quine, Davidson supposes that the answers to these questions will constitute a more-or-less complete philosophical account of meaning. However, unlike Quine, who took for granted that the hard issue here was confined to the second question – Can determinately correct translation manuals ever be found? – Davidson focussed equal attention on an aspect of the first one – How could interpretations of the infinitely many complex expressions of a language be derived (as they surely must be) from finitely many assumptions about the meanings of the primitive terms?[1] What

---

[1] For Quine's account of meaning and translation see his 1962; for Davidson's views see the essays in Davidson 1984 – especially 'Truth and Meaning' (first published: Davidson 1967).

form would our hypotheses about the meanings of someone's words and sentences have to take in order that the latter be deducible from the former? And for that matter, how does the understanding we have of our *own* language derive from our understanding of its basic elements.

Davidson's approach to his new problem was ingenious and appealing: – we should solve it by piggy-backing on Tarski's work on truth.[2] For Tarski showed us how the truth conditions of various formalised sentences could be deduced, in predicate logic, from premises specifying the referents of names and simple predicates, and from further premises specifying, for each connective, how the referent (or truth-value) of any complex that is formed with it depends on the referents (or truth-values) of the connected expressions. Therefore, if we identify a sentence's possessing the meaning it does with its having a certain truth condition, and if we identify a word's possessing the meaning it does with its having a certain referent (or, in the case of a connective, with the fact about how the truth-values/referents of the complexes formed with it depend on the truth-values/referents of the connected expressions), then Tarski-style deductions of truth conditions become precisely what we were looking for: namely, derivations of sentence-meanings on the basis of assumptions about word-meanings.

Consider for example how to arrive in such a way at an interpretation of the Italian sentence 'Gira Marte'. We would begin with the three semantic premises:

The name 'Marte' refers-in-formal-Italian to Mars[3]

The predicate 'gira(x)' is true-in-formal-Italian of k $\leftrightarrow$ k rotates

The result of applying a predicate to a name is true-in-formal-Italian $\leftrightarrow$ the predicate is true-in-formal-Italian of the referent-in-formal-Italian of the name

And we also have the syntactic premise

The result of applying 'gira(x)' to 'Marte' is 'gira(Marte)'

---

[2] To the other problem – that of how we might *verify* a given interpretation – Davidson's solution is similar to Quine's. The method based on his Principle of Charity differs only in detail from Quine's strategy of radical translation.

[3] The route through 'formal Italian' is necessary because Tarskian deductions of truth conditions can be carried out only for sentences in some logically regimented (i.e. formalised) part of the language. Other sentences may then be dealt with by attributing to them the same truth conditions as their formalisations.

From these assumptions we would infer that

'gira(Marte)' is true-in-formal-Italian ↔ Mars rotates

Then we would invoke the fact that

The formal Italian, 'gira(Marte)', gives the meaning of the
ordinary Italian sentence, 'Gira Marte'

which puts us in a position to conclude that

'Gira Marte' is true-in-Italian ↔ Mars rotates

More generally, Davidson conjectured that for *every* sentence of a
natural language we could deduce and explain why it means what
it does by explaining, along Tarskian lines, why its logical formalisation (or regimented equivalent) has the truth condition that it
does. And this idea became widely accepted, instigating several
decades of 'normal science' in semantics.

The research projects engendered by the Davidsonian para-
digm fell into two groups. First it was necessary to show how the
strategy could be applied to *all* sentences, including those built
with devices that Tarski did not investigate. How, for example,
might we deduce the truth conditions of sentences containing
adverbs, or that-clauses, or attributive adjectives, or conditional-
probability constructions, on the basis of premises concerning
the referents of their words? To that end, how could such
sentences be formalised in first order predicate logic? Over the
last thirty years, ingenious solutions have been found to several
problems of this sort, although many kinds of sentence still
remain intractable.

The second set of issues that needed to be addressed included
various foundational questions. For instance, does the truth
condition of a sentence in fact suffice to determine its meaning?
In other words, is there any reading of 's is true *if and only if* p' in
which it will be strong enough to ensure 's means that p'?
Considerable efforts to find or devise such a construal have not
yet produced an acceptable one.[4]

---

[4] One sometimes hears it said, on behalf of Davidson, that he was not really attempting to analyse, or even to explicate, 's means that p', but rather to get along without this
obscure notion and to make do with the relatively unproblematic 's is true if and only if
p'. But remember that the problem he set was to specify which assumptions about a person
would enable us to tell what beliefs his assertive utterances are expressing – i.e to say what
he means. So if the answer, roughly speaking, is that these assumptions must concern the
'truth conditions' of his utterances, then it is obligatory to face up to the challenge of artic-
ulating precisely what sort of truth-conditional claim about a sentence would amount to a

Moreover, does a natural language sentence in fact have the same meaning as the best formulation one can give of it in predicate logic? For example, is it plausible that 'John might win' has just the same meaning as '$(\exists x)$[PossWorld(x) & Wins(John, x)]', and that the sense of 'Mary is walking slowly' is identical to that of '$(\exists x)$[Walking(x) & By$(x$, Mary) & Slow(x)]'? No doubt the members of such pairs necessarily have the same truth value; but the structural and semantic differences between them are nonetheless so great that one might well wonder whether they could count as exact synonyms of one another.

The expectation that these technical and foundational difficulties will eventually be overcome derives largely from the conviction that there is no decent alternative to the Davidsonian truth-theoretic perspective, and therefore that it *must* be more-or-less right. It seems to me, however, that there *is* a good alternative – a 'deflationary' alternative – whose correctness would undermine the purpose of the Davidsonian research programme and make it unnecessary to swallow its various implausible commitments.

This alternative is deflationary, for its basic idea is that Davidson's problem (of how we might derive interpretations of complex expressions) has a trivial solution. This solution assumes the principle of compositionality (that the meaning of a complex is determined by the meanings of its elements and by its syntactic structure); but it involves no explication of meaning (e.g. in terms of truth conditions) and hence offers no explanation of *why* the principle of compositionality holds.

For illustration, look again at how we might reach an interpretation of 'Gira Marte'. We might begin with premises specifying the meanings of its primitives:

'Marte' in Italian means the same as *our* 'Mars'

'gira_' in Italian means the same as *our* '_rotates'

Then, from the principle of compositionality, we can infer

view of what it means. It seems clear that Davidson himself *does* face up to this challenge, and that he is responsible for some of the attempts to meet it. For example, there is the idea that 's is true if and only if p' be understood as 'It is a law of nature that (s is true ↔ p)', or that it be understood as 'It follows from any truth theory verified via the Principle of Charity that (s is true ↔ p)'. A problem with all such construals – which take the form '□(s is true ↔ p)' – is that if the analysans is satisfied, and if we can find some 'q' (as it would seem we always can) not synonymous with 'p' yet such that □(p↔q), then even though s does not mean that q, we can nonetheless infer that □(s is true ↔ q).

The result of applying 'gira_' to 'Marte' in Italian means the same as the result of *our* applying '_rotates' to 'Mars'

And finally, given the syntactic facts

The result of applying 'gira_' to 'Marte' = 'Gira Marte'

The result of applying '_rotates' to 'Mars' = 'Mars rotates'

we can deduce the interpretation

'Gira Marte' in Italian means the same as *our* 'Mars rotates'

And, in general, whenever some foreign expression is constructed by imposing a certain combinatorial procedure on certain words (including schemata), then we can interpret it in our language with the expression that results from imposing exactly the same procedure on synonyms of those words.[5]

If this sort of approach will do, then Davidson's programme, and all its attendant difficulties, can be put behind us. We can abandon the desperate struggle to find a conception of 'truth condition' sufficiently strong to capture meaning. We will then be able to avoid the problematic commitment to cram every natural language construction into the narrow mould of predicate logic. And in that case there will be no need to claim, rather implausibly as we have seen, that the predicate logic formalisation of a natural language sentence will perfectly preserve its meaning. What a relief!

But *will* the deflationary approach do? Davidson himself was always aware of it. So it is worth our while to examine his reasons for rejecting the idea and to consider how persuasive they are.

In the first place, he argues (in his essay 'Radical Interpretation') that a manual of translation does not fully convey meanings, and so cannot amount to an interpretation. For one can be told that two expressions should be inter-translated – i.e. that they have the same meaning as each other – without being given any understanding of either one of them.[6]

However, the problem we were set was to specify the assumptions

---

[5] Notice that although we translate a foreign expression with one of ours that has the same structure (i.e. that results from the same combinatorial procedure), the *order* of synonymous words need not be the same. For the basic elements of a language include *schemata* (e.g. 'gira_' and '_rotates'). Therefore word order will partially derive from where the 'slots' in these schemata are located. Thus an identity of combinatorial procedure is quite consistent with a difference of word order.

[6] Davidson 1984, pp. 129–130.

we might make that would enable us to interpret a foreign language. And one good answer is that a correct manual of translation will do the trick. Granted, the information it provides will suffice only given an unexplained further fact – namely that we understand our own language. But notice that no alternative account – no alternative view of which explicit assumptions will yield interpretations of foreign speech – could escape something like this critique. For any such assumptions would presumably need a language for their articulation (even in thought) – a language which would have to be understood. So, for example, the explicit assumption that 'Marte' refers to Mars requires that we already understand some term that refers to Mars – and this understanding remains unexplained. The obvious moral to draw is that we can understand a language only if we have available to us certain terms (possibly within a different language) whose meanings we know *implicitly* – that is, not in virtue of *articulated assumptions* about those terms, but in virtue of *facts* about what they mean, i.e. facts concerning how they are deployed. But leaving that moral aside until later, the point remains that although a translation manual can supply interpretations only relative to our understanding of our own language, the same can be said of any alternative view one might have of which explicit assumptions would work.

But, for the sake of argument, let us bow to Davidson's objection – at least to the letter of it – and take up his challenge to specify what knowledge (whether explicit or implicit) would suffice to understand a language (whether someone else's or one's own). This creates no particular difficulty for the deflationary strategy, because it is a simple matter to present the approach in terms of meaning-facts rather than translation-facts. We can begin by adopting the convention that each capitalised English expression be a name of the meaning of the original lower-case expression: thus 'Mars' means MARS, '_rotates' means ROTATES(x), 'Mars rotates' means MARS ROTATES, and so on. Then we can invoke the principle of compositionality in a peculiarly Fregean form – namely, that the result of applying one term to others (to produce a complex expression) *means* the result of applying the meaning of the first term to the meanings of the others. In that case, we can infer that both 'Mars rotates' and 'Gira Marte' mean the result of applying the function ROTATES(x) to the argument MARS, therefore that these sentences mean the same thing, and therefore – since, by our convention, 'Mars rotates' means MARS ROTATES – that 'Gira Marte' also means MARS ROTATES. At the beginning of his 'Truth and Meaning' Davidson dismisses that particular way of trying to give a

> . . . useful account of how the meanings of sentences depend upon the meanings of the words (or other structural features) that compose them. Ask, for example, for the meaning of 'Theatetus flies'. A Fregean answer might go something like this: given the meaning of 'Theatetus' as argument, the meaning of 'flies' yields the meaning of 'Theatetus flies' as value. The vacuity of this argument is obvious. We wanted to know what the meaning of 'Theatetus flies' is; it is no progress to be told that it is the meaning of 'Theatetus flies'. This much we knew before any theory was in sight. In the bogus account just given, talk of the structure of the sentence and of the meanings of words was idle, for it played no role in producing the given description of the meaning of the sentence.[7]

But the Fregean answer does *not* merely apply the logical law of identity to the meaning of 'Theatetus flies' – which would indeed be of no interest. Rather, it incorporates the principle of compositionality – a non-trivial principle – by maintaining that the meaning of the result of applying a function-expression to certain argument-expressions equals the result of applying the meaning of the function to the meanings of its arguments. It is therefore not at all true that our assumptions about the structure of a sentence, and about the meanings of its words, will play no role in our characterisation of the meaning of that sentence.

What *is* true is that we have not *identified* (in some peculiarly direct sense) the meaning of 'Theatetus flies'. We have specified it merely via the construction description, 'the result of applying FLIES(x) to THEATETUS'; but we have not said what that result is, what the description describes.[8] However, a vital aspect of the deflationary attitude is to question whether there is a need for any such deeper, more immediate characterisation of that meaning. Consider, by analogy, the number we designate with the term '15' – or, to spell out what this notation means, 'the sum of 10 and 5'. We

---

[7] *Ibid.*, p. 20.
[8] For a sympathetic elaboration of Davidson's complaint that the deflationary approach fails to specify directly what the meanings of complexes are, see Higginbotham 1999.

would regard it as explanatorily otiose, indeed downright bizarre, to insist on some more direct identification of the entity described either in that or some other way. Arithmetic and its applications call for no more than such descriptions. And the same goes in semantics for construction characterisations of the meanings of complex expressions.

It is also true, as a consequence, that we are not attempting to *explain* the phenomenon of compositionality. We are not associating specific, independently identifiable entities with the meanings of 'Theatetus', 'flies', and 'Theatetus flies', and then proceeding to show how the latter entity is determined by the former ones. The Fregean principle merely articulates the thesis of compositionality without explaining it. However, it was no part of the original Davidsonian problem to explain compositionality. Indeed one might well suppose that compositionality is explanatorily basic – simply not derivable from anything more fundamental. The original problem was to show how interpretations of words, together with assumptions about the structures of complex expressions, could yield interpretations of those complexes. And for this purpose we need merely assume that compositionality *does* hold. No explanation of *why* it holds is required.[9]

A little later in the same article, Davidson makes a further criticism of the deflationary approach:

> This is the place to scotch another hopeful thought. Suppose we have a satisfactory theory of syntax for our language, consisting of an effective method of telling, for an arbitrary expression, whether or not it is independently meaningful (i.e. a sentence), and assume as usual that this involves viewing each sentence as composed, in allowable ways, out of elements drawn from a fixed finite stock of atomic syntactic elements (roughly, words). The hopeful thought is that syntax, so conceived, will yield semantics when a dictionary giving the meaning of each syntactic atom is added. Hopes will be dashed, however, if semantics is to comprise a theory of meaning in our sense, for *knowledge of the structural characteristics that make for meaningfulness in a sentence, plus knowledge of the meanings of the ultimate parts, does not add up to knowledge of what a sentence means.* The point is easily illustrated by belief sentences. Their syntax

---

[9] For further discussion and defence of the deflationary view of compositionality, see Horwich 1997, reprinted as ch. 7 of Horwich 1998.

is relatively unproblematic. Yet, adding a dictionary does not touch the standard semantic problem, which is that *we cannot account for even as much as the truth conditions of such sentences* on the basis of what we know of the meanings of the words in them.[10]

The central point here is that knowledge of the syntax of a sentence – for example, a belief attribution – plus knowledge of what its words mean, will not enable us to infer the sentence's truth condition. But I can find no construal of this claim in which it constitutes a good objection to deflationism.

Does it mean that the imagined knowledge about a sentence, s, cannot yield any conclusion of the form 's is true if and only if p'? If so the claim is mistaken. Once we have determined, via the deflationary approach described and illustrated above, that a sentence means JOHN BELIEVES THAT DOGS BARK, we may straightaway conclude that it is true if and only if John believes that dogs bark. We simply invoke the schema 's means P → (s is true ↔ p)'.

So, perhaps Davidson's claim is meant to be that the proposed account does not yield a *compositional* account of truth conditions – a deduction of them from premises about the referential properties of words. In that case, our response is that it is precisely the point of the deflationary approach to question the need for such an account. For we can interpret foreign speakers perfectly well without it, merely on the basis of the unexplained principle that meaning is compositional.[11]

Finally, Davidson's point might be that knowledge of the syntax of a sentence, plus knowledge of what its words mean, do not together suffice for us to be able to say, for a variety of conditions, whether the sentence would be true in each of those conditions. And it is indeed clear that in order to decide if a sentence, 'A', would be true in certain specified circumstances, C, one must invoke relevant rules of inference to determine whether the sentence does or does not follow from how those circumstances are characterised: – i.e. to determine whether 'A' does or does not

---

[10] Davidson 1984, p. 21 (my emphasis).

[11] Note that the quoted passage appears before Davidson's presentation of his own solution to the problem of how interpretation is possible; it occurs in the context of critical discussions of various initial attempts to solve it. His arguments that these attempts all fail are intended to give support to the truth-theoretic alternative solution which he goes on to articulate. But in that case these arguments cannot legitimately presuppose that we already accept that solution.

follow from 'C'. But, notice that the same would be true from within a Davidsonian framework. Even if we are given a truth-theoretic account of the meaning of 'A', there will be a need to consult logical rules in order to settle whether "A" would be true in circumstances C – i.e. whether it follows from 'C'. One might think that an advantage of the Davidsonian approach – stemming from the fact that it deals, in the first instance, with regimented or formalised sentences – is that the needed rules are well-established; they are the standard rules of predicate logic. Whereas it is relatively mysterious what rules of inference, applying to structurally-explicit *natural* language sentences, are available to be invoked by the deflationist. In fact, however, *both* approaches must confront this question. For remember that the Davidsonian is compelled to recognise the existence of 'transformation principles' associating ordinary sentences with sentences in a regimented part (or formalised extension) of the language; and such principles do not differ substantially from rules of deduction. Therefore, a commitment to there being ordinary language inference rules is necessary on either strategy.[12]

I conclude that Davidson's resistance to the deflationary view of compositionality is unjustified. In order to interpret the expressions of a language it suffices to assume that meaning is compositional. There is no need to explain that fact by analysing sentence-meanings in terms of truth conditions. Indeed, there is no reason to suppose that it *can* be explained. Consequently, we are left with no motivation at all for embracing the truth-theoretic approach.

---

[12] Once we abandon the idea of explaining compositionality in truth-theoretic terms then *one* influential reason for identifying semantic structures with expressions of 1ˢᵗ order predicate logic is undermined. Indeed, we might also begin to wonder about the need to draw any distinction at all between semantic and syntactic structures. Let me stress, however, that these further anti-Davidsonian speculations are not *integral* to deflationism about compositionality. Deflationism implies that we should take them seriously. But their correctness will hinge on whether the phenomena (including inferences and structural ambiguities) that are standardly explained by invoking predicate-logic semantic structures can be better explained without them. The above paragraph suggests that the prospects for finding such better explanations within a non-standard 'syntactic semantics' are by no means negligible. For we see that standard explanations (based merely on predicate logic) of inferences are often radically incomplete and that syntactically-oriented rules of logic are also needed. But an attempt to settle these issues would take us far beyond the scope of this paper. The central anti-Davidsonian claim here is quite independent of them. It is simply this: that however the semantic structure of a sentence is articulated – whether it be in terms of a predicate logic structure, a syntactic structure, or something else – the meaning of the sentence need not, and should not, be derived truth-theoretically; for it can be obtained, as illustrated above, merely on the basis of assumptions about its structure, the meanings of its words, and the principle of compositionality.

Besides Davidson, two other philosophers who have drawn overly strong conclusions from the compositionality of meaning are Jerry Fodor and Ernie Lepore. In a series of papers and books they argue that

. . . compositionality is the sovereign test for theories of lexical meaning. So hard is this test to pass, we think, that it filters out practically all of the theories of lexical meaning that are current in either philosophy or cognitive science. Among the casualties are, for example, the theory that lexical meanings are statistical structures (like stereotypes); the theory that the meaning of a word is its use; the theory that knowing the meaning of (at least some) words requires having a recognitional capacity for (at least some) of the things that it applies to; and the theory that knowing the meaning of a word requires knowing criteria for applying it.[13]

Their strategy of argument is very simple. Suppose someone maintains that the meaning of a word (or the content of a mentalese term) is engendered by its inferential role (or associated stereotype, or recognitional capacity – or to put it schematically, by its G-property). To refute any such claim, Fodor and Lepore deploy the following objection: – Meanings are compositional; G-properties are not (– Here they plug in one of the targeted theories, e.g. inferential roles, stereotypes, criteria, . . .); therefore meanings aren't engendered by G-properties. Or, more explicitly:

(1) A complex's meaning what it does is determined by its structure and the meanings of its words.

(2) A complex's G-property is *not* determined by its structure and the G-properties of its words. (This is supported by examples: – e.g. the stereotype associated with 'pet fish' is not determined by the stereotypical pet and the stereotypical fish).

(3) Therefore, the meaning of an expression is not engendered by its G-property.

But there is a hole in this line of thought. No matter what is substituted for 'G', the argument is valid only in the presence of a further premise: the following Uniformity Assumption

[13] See Fodor & Lepore 2001, p. 59 of this volume. See also Fodor 1998; Fodor & Lepore 1991a; Fodor & Lepore 1996; and Fodor & Lepore 1991b.

If the meanings of words are engendered by their G-properties, then so are the meanings of complexes.

Without that assumption the most one can conclude from (1) and (2) is that *either* the meanings of words aren't engendered by their G-properties, *or* the meanings of complexes aren't. Thus it would be perfectly coherent for someone to deny the Uniformity Assumption and maintain that whereas the meanings of *words* are engendered by their inferential roles (say), the meanings of complexes are constituted in some other way.[14]

For example, it might be supposed that

The word 'pet' means what it does in virtue of the fact that IR_1('pet')
The word 'fish' means what it does in virtue of the fact that IR_2('fish')
The schema '*a n*' means what it does in virtue of the fact that IR_3('*a n*')

but that

The sentence 'pet fish' means what it does *not* in virtue of its possessing some further inferential role, IR_4; but, rather, in virtue of its being the result of substituting words meaning what 'pet' and 'fish' do into a schema meaning what '*a n*' does

This would be an instance of the deflationary view of compositionality – to take such facts about how the meanings of complex expressions are engendered to be explanatorily basic. From this perspective we should resist the impulse to begin by identifying the kind of fact in virtue of which (i) complexes and (ii) lexical items, mean what they do; to continue by proving that the former facts will indeed be determined by the latter; and to conclude that the compositionality of complex expressions has thereby been explained. That is the inflationary aspiration embodied in Davidson's truth-theoretic semantics; and the same mistake (in the form of their Uniformity Assumption) vitiates the strategy of argument deployed by Fodor and Lepore.

[14] A slightly different interpretation of the argument offered by Fodor and Lepore sees it directed against various claims about the identity of meaning *entities* (e.g. that DOG = such-and-such inferential role) rather than, as I have assumed, against theories of how meaning-*properties* are constituted (e.g. that w means DOG in virtue of having such-and-such inferential role). But the same objection can be made against this variant. Namely, that we need not identify the meanings of *complex* expressions with the same kinds of thing with which we identify the meanings of *words*.

In subsequent defence of that assumption, and hence of their overall strategy, Fodor and Lepore cite what they aptly call 'the principle of *reverse* compositionality', according to which the fact that a complex means what it does determines the structure of that complex and the meanings of its constituents. This principle implies, for example, that an expression can mean PET FISH *only* if it is constructed from terms meaning PET and FISH. Their line of thought is then

(1) that compositionality and reverse compositionality are both plausible;

(2) that the conjunction of these facts is best explained by supposing that the meanings of words are *components* of (i.e. present in) the meanings of the complex expressions they form; and

(3) that this suggests that the Uniformity Assumption is indeed correct.[15]

Now one might accept their first step – at least with respect to our most fine-grained conception of meaning[16]. And one might also accept the second step – at least if it is taken to say that the meaning of a complex 'contains' (in some suitable non-spatial sense) all and *only* the meanings of its component words. But surely (2) does not lead to (3). For one might naturally construe (2) as implying that the meanings of complexes are ordered *sets* whose members are the meanings of words. But then word meanings – which are presumably *not* sets – would be very different kinds of entity from the meanings of complexes. And in that case one would expect the kind of property in virtue of which a complex means what it does to be quite different from the kind of property in virtue of which a word means what it does. One might then very naturally agree with the deflationist that the property that is responsible for a *complex's* meaning what it does *isn't* a use or inferential role, *isn't* a prototype, and *isn't* a recognitional capacity – but is rather the property of being constructed in a certain way from words with certain uses, or associated prototypes, or

---

[15] See Fodor & Lepore 2001, this volume, pp. 59–75.

[16] In Horwich 1997, I suggest that the meaning-property of a complex expression is *constituted* by its being constructed in a certain way from words with certain meanings. And this would entail reverse compositionality. But here I have refrained from making the constitution claim, thereby leaving it open whether reverse compositionality holds.

recognitional capacities, . . ., or whatever other characteristic one takes to engender the meanings of words.[17]

Not that there is nothing to choose amongst these alternatives; but the need to accommodate the two compositionality principles won't be what decides the issue. The constraint we need in order to obtain a good theory of lexical meaning comes, not from the *compositionality* of meaning, but rather from the *use import* of meaning: – namely, that the overall use of a complex is explained by the meanings of its words and how they are combined. From this constraint we can infer that the property responsible for a word's having the meaning it does is the property that (in conjunction with other factors, including the meaning-constituting properties of other words) can best account for the inferential character, and the circumstances of acceptance and rejection, of all the various sentences in which it appears. And this points us in the direction of a *use* theory of word meaning. For, quite plausibly, a word's conformity with certain *core regularities* of use is the property that explains it *overall* use. More specifically, we might well be led to conclude that the meaning of a word derives from the fact that certain specified sentences containing it are accepted underived (in certain specified conditions).[18] But this is not to subscribe to a use theory of *sentence* meaning. Therefore there is no obliga-

[17] Although Fodor and Lepore believe that their Uniformity Assumption is correct and that it can be supported in the way just discussed, they maintain (in this volume) that neither it, nor the argument of which it is a part, are really needed in order to see that compositionality substantially constrains the nature of lexical meaning. For they think that there is a separate line of thought that yields this conclusion: viz.

1) Anyone who understands certain complex expressions (e.g. 'Flounders swim' and 'John snores') must also understand other expressions built from the same elements (e.g. 'Flounders snore'). ('systematicity')
2) Therefore, the meaning of a term does not depend on the complex expression in which it appears. ('context-independence')
3) But the stereotype associated with the word 'swim' in 'Flounders swim' is not the same as the stereotype associated with that word in 'John swims'
4) Therefore the meaning of 'swim' is not engendered by an associated stereotype.
But note (a) that any alert defender of the stereotype theory of meaning will simply deny premise 3 and will maintain that his theory, properly stated, is that the stereotype associated with the isolated word 'swim', whatever it may be, is the meaning of that word *wherever* it occurs; (b) that even if the above argument were persuasive it could tell against only the stereotype theory, but would have no bearing on any of the other accounts of lexical meaning (e.g. the use theory) that were alleged by Fodor and Lepore to be precluded by compositionality; and (c) the argument does not really hinge on compositionality, but rather on context-independence – so it cannot be presented as a justification of their claim that *compositionality* filters out virtually all theories of lexical meaning.

[18] For a sustained explanation and defence of this form of the use theory of meaning, see Horwich 1998, Ch. 3.

tion to show how the *core* uses of sentences (whatever that might be!) are determined by the core uses of words – and thereby to *explain* compositionality. Our only obligation – but this is an fairly onerous one – is to discover which particular basic acceptance properties of words will provide the best explanations of their overall uses (i.e. of the uses of all the sentences containing them). As for the *meanings* of those sentences, they derive from their construction out of words with certain uses.[19] And nothing need be said about how and why.

Let me end with a word on understanding one's *own* language. In order that I understand for example the English sentence 'Mars rotates', it is conceptually (a priori) necessary and sufficient for me to *know* (in some sense) what it means – specifically, that it means MARS ROTATES. But it cannot be my *explicit* knowledge of this fact that constitutes my understanding of the sentence; for that would be too easy; I can explicitly infer it merely from the capitalising convention for naming meanings. Rather, the needed knowledge is *implicit*[20]– it consists in the fact that what 'Mars rotates' means in my idiolect resembles its meaning in English. And that resemblance derives, in turn, from the fact that the basic uses of the words 'Mars' and '_rotates' (and their mode of combination) are similar in my idiolect and in the public language.[21] Consequently, if someone implicitly knows the meanings of the

[19] It might be thought that I have skated over the *real* problem of compositionality – which is to show how it might be so much as possible for properties assigned to individual words (e.g. basic regularities in their use) to explain the overall usage of all the unlimited number of sentences that can be made from them. But this is also a pseudo-puzzle. For the law of use associated with a function term will specify the usage of any results of applying it to other expressions. E.g., the meaning-constituting property of 'and' is that there be an underived tendency to infer 'p and q' from 'p' and 'q' and *vice versa*. Therefore, just as laws governing the behaviour of electrons, protons, etc., explain the properties of whatever is made out of them, it is trivial that the basic uses of words will have consequences for the usage of all the complexes into which they enter.

[20] Fodor and Lepore stress the importance of distinguishing, on the one hand, the contrast between *occurrent* and *dispositional* mental states and, on the other hand, the contrast between *conscious* and *unconscious* states. And they think that my use of 'explicit' and 'implicit' oscillates confusingly between these alternatives. But in fact I am pointing to a *third* contrast by means of that terminology. Explicit commitments are articulated – i.e. spelled out in the 'belief box' – whereas implicit commitments are not. E.g. my implicit knowledge that 'Mars rotates' means, in my idiolect, MARS ROTATES consists merely in the *fact* that it has that meaning. Therefore explicit commitments may be either conscious or unconscious, and either occurrent or dispositional; and the same may be said of implicit commitments.

[21] The emphasis on *resemblance* between idiolectal and public language meanings is intended to explain how understanding an expression is a matter of degree. By 'basic use in the public language' I mean basic use by the experts.

elements of a sentence of his language – whether it be a sentence-type or a sentence-token – and also knows how those elements are combined, he thereby satisfies the condition for understanding the whole. There is no need for any inference, or for any other sort of process, to take him from those antecedent items of knowledge to the state of understanding the sentence.

Contrary to Fodor and Lepore[22] it is no objection to these theses that one may come across a sentence-token (e.g. 'Dogs dogs dog dog dogs'), be given information about its structure (e.g. '[[Dogs$_N$ [dogs$_N$ dog$_V$]]$_{NP}$[dog$_V$ dogs$_N$]$_{VP}$]$_S$'), know what the words mean, and yet still not understand that sentence. For, the knowledge required for understanding a *word* does not amount to having some piece of *explicit* information about its meaning (e.g. that 'dog' means the same as 'chien') but is rather a matter of know-*how* (i.e. a mastery of its use). And similarly, the required knowledge of structure cannot take the form of some theoretical characterisation of it, but must also be implicit and manifested in use (e.g. being disposed to infer 'Certain dogs dog dogs'). Once *this* sort of knowledge of word meanings and sentence structure is obtained, then understanding the sentence is guaranteed.

Nor is it reasonable to object that since understanding is a form of knowledge, and since knowledge yields further knowledge only by inference, our understanding of complex expressions *must* result from inference. This *conclusion* can't be right; because, regarding our understanding of the language of thought (whether it be an ordinary language or universal mentalese), there would be no language in which to conduct the alleged inferences. Moreover, the *argument* for that conclusion isn't right; because it is only for *articulated* (though perhaps unconscious) knowledge – i.e. spelled out in the language of thought – that transitions between states of knowledge are likely to be mediated by inference; but understanding is *implicit* knowledge.

Finally, it is not relevant to point out that if, as a matter of empirical fact, we think in a universal mentalese, then understanding a token of an ordinary sentence will require translating it into that mental language – a process which might involve explicit (yet unconscious) inferences. This is beside the point; for, even if inferences are involved, they will enter merely into how we grasp the *structure* of the sentence token (and maybe into how we learned the meanings of its words). They will *not* be employed in the move from

[22] See Fodor & Lepore 2001, pp. 59–75.

that grasp, and from our knowledge of word meanings, to our understanding of the token. For there is no such move. To see this once again, suppose that properly understanding a token of 'Mars rotates' is empirically constituted by unconsciously translating it into a specific sentence, 'm', of mentalese – a sentence consisting in a certain structure imposed on certain mentalese terms. Now imagine someone who happens to translate 'Mars rotates' into a *different* mentalese sentence 'm*' – i.e. his understanding is defective. Then it must be (as a matter of conceptual necessity) that either the *structure* of 'm' differs from the structure of 'm*', or that the *terms* making up these mentalese sentences are not all the same. In other words, either our subject hasn't on this occasion understood 'Mars' or '_rotates', or he hasn't grasped how those words have been combined. Thus once the meanings of the words in a token, and the way these words are combined, have been properly – i.e. implicitly – identified, there is nothing more to be done. The conditions for understanding have been met.[23]

The Graduate Center
The City University of New York
New York, USA
PHorwich@gc.cuny.edu

References

Davidson, D. (1967). 'Truth and Meaning'. *Synthese* 17, 304–323.
Davidson, D. (1984). *Inquiries into Truth and Interpretation*. Oxford: Clarendon Press.
Fodor, J. (1998). 'There Are No Recognitional Concepts; Not Even RED', in E. Villanueva, ed., *Philosophical Issues*, Vol. 9. Atascadero, Ca.: Ridgeview. Reprinted in Fodor (1998b) *In Critical Condition*. Cambridge, Mass.: MIT Press, 35–48.
Fodor, J. and E. Lepore (1991a). 'Why Meaning (Probably) Isn't Conceptual Role'. *Mind and Language* 6, 329–43.
Fodor, J. and E. Lepore (1991b). *Holism*. Oxford: Blackwell.
Fodor, J. and E. Lepore (1996). 'The Pet Fish and the Red Herring; Why Concepts Aren't Prototypes'. *Cognition* 52, 243–276.
Fodor, J. and E. Lepore (2001). 'Why Compositionality Won't Go Away'. *Ratio* 14, 350–368. Reprinted in this volume: Ch. 5, 58–76.
Higginbotham, J. (1999). 'A Perspective on Truth and Meaning', in L. Hahn, ed., *The Philosophy of Donald Davidson*. La Salle, Illinois: Open Court.
Horwich, P. (1997). 'The Composition of Meanings'. *Philosophical Review* 106, 503–31. Reprinted as Ch.7, Horwich (1998).
Horwich, P. (1998). *Meaning*. Oxford: Oxford University Press.
Quine, W.V. (1962). *Word and Object*. Cambridge, Mass.: MIT Press.

---

[23] I would like to thank Jim Edwards, Jerry Fodor, Ernie Lepore, Stephen Neale, Barry C. Smith, and Mark Sainsbury for helpful discussions of the issues treated in this paper.

CHAPTER 7

TWO WAYS TO SMOKE A CIGARETTE

R. M. Sainsbury

Abstract
In the early part of the paper, I attempt to explain a dispute
between two parties who endorse the compositionality of language
but disagree about its implications: Paul Horwich, and Jerry Fodor
and Ernest Lepore. In the remainder of the paper, I challenge the
thesis on which they are agreed, that compositionality can be taken
for granted. I suggest that it is not clear what compositionality
involves nor whether it obtains. I consider some kinds of apparent
counterexamples, and compositionalist responses to them in terms
of covert indexicality and unspecific meanings. I argue that the last
option is the best for most of the cases I consider. I conclude by
stressing, as against Horwich and Fodor and Lepore, that the
appropriate question concerns the extent to which compositionality obtains in a natural language, rather than whether it obtains or
not, so that the answer is essentially messy, requiring detailed
consideration of a wide range of examples.

1. Introduction

We understand sentences thanks to understanding the words of
which they are composed and how these words are arranged.
That is a truism. It has been held to support some 'principle of
compositionality', but as soon as one tries to formulate such a
principle, one moves away from truism. Identifying and defend-
ing a correct principle of compositionality raises many central
issues in philosophy of language:

1) Principles of compositionality typically relate to meanings,
   rather than to understanding, for example: 'the meanings
   of complex expressions . . . are constructed from the meanings of the less complex expressions . . . that are their
   constituents' (Fodor and Lepore 2001, p. 58–9). Such principles appear seriously committed to meanings as entities,
   which the truism is not.

It is not to be assumed that meanings are entities, or that we can correctly extend the truism about understanding to meanings.

2) Principles of compositionality appear to assume that simple expressions have meaning 'in isolation', independently of their occurrence in complexes.

This seems to be inconsistent with Frege's 'context principle': 'never to ask for the meaning of a word in isolation, but only in the context of a proposition' (Frege 1884, p. x).

3) If understanding a word is *defined* in terms of appreciating its contribution to whole sentences, the compositionality of understanding may be trivial.

4) The notion of 'word', 'constituent' or 'simple expression' requires spelling out, to avoid holding that there is a 'gnat' in 'indignant' or that 'nails' is a constituent of 'John ails', and to do justice to so-called 'idioms' ('kick the bucket'). This suggests that a serious principle of compositionality needs to be relative to a syntactic description of the language. If this description is constrained by the need to respect compositionality, circularity threatens.

5) Whereas the truism says we understand sentences 'thanks to' understanding the words in them, principles of compositionality generally see the meanings of the simple elements, together with the significance of their arrangement, as *sufficient* for fixing the meanings of sentences.

6) The truism speaks of understanding sentences, by which I mean sentence types. One might wish to consider compositionality principles which relate to utterances (tokens): the use of a sentence on a specific occasion.

This raises questions about the role of extra-semantic knowledge in such context-based 'pragmatic' activities as determining reference, resolving ambiguity, filling in ellipsis, adjusting for speaker error (e.g. malapropism), and identifying 'non-literal' uses (metaphor, irony etc).

I begin (in §2) by discussing a dispute about compositionality in which the correctness of some principle of this kind is taken for granted. The disputants are Paul Horwich on the one hand, and, on the other, Jerry Fodor and Ernest Lepore (see Horwich 2001, Fodor and Lepore 2001 (F&L)). In §3 I offer a minimal principle of compositionality, and in the remainder of the paper (§4–6) I consider counterexamples to it which relate to issues in group (6).

2. Does compositionality constrain accounts of the meaning of words?

The parties to the dispute agree that some principle of compositionality holds.[1] The crucial disagreement appears to be whether the principle places any constraints on what the meanings of words can be. In earlier work, Horwich had written: 'the compositionality of meaning imposes no constraint at all on how the meaning properties of *words* are constituted' (Horwich 1998, p. 154). Reading the phrase 'how the meaning properties of words are constituted' as amounting to 'what the meanings of words are', Fodor and Lepore express surprise, and protest that 'compositionality must rule out at least *some* theories about what word meanings are' (Fodor and Lepore 2001, p. 59). I think they are wrong to read Horwich in this way, and that Horwich's enterprise is so different from theirs that it is easy to overestimate the common ground between them.

As I see it, Horwich's main concern in *Meaning* is to say what it is for a language to mean what it does. This calls for some kind of reductive or explanatory connection between what various elements of the language mean and the activities of speakers upon which this fact supervenes. This is a quite different project from that of giving a theory of meaning for a language: a finite statement from which follows a specification of the meaning of every sentence of the language. A theory of meaning, in this sense, does not say anything at all about how psychological features of speakers provide a supervenience base for the facts the theory states. Similarly, an account of how this supervenience relation works does not as such include a theory of meaning.[2]

---

[1] Fodor and Lepore's version was cited above. Horwich writes that a problem is to be solved by invoking 'the principle of compositionality (that the meaning of a complex is determined by the meanings of its elements and by its syntactic structure)', Horwich 2001, p. 80.

[2] Something like the contrast I insist on here is drawn by Stalnaker (1997) in the terms 'descriptive semantics' (theory of meaning) versus 'foundational semantics' (specification of supervenience base). Employing it, one could say that Horwich claims that foundational semantics, while respecting compositionality, has no implications for what descriptive semantics says about lexical meaning, whereas F&L claim that compositionality has consequences for which accounts of lexical meaning may rightly figure in descriptive semantics. These claims are consistent. Inconsistency arises if one party claims the other's project is irrelevant.

Horwich addresses the supervenience question in terms of how words and certain simple syntactic structures (like NP+VP) are used. He then relies on the principle of compositionality to show that his work is done: given that the meanings of complexes are determined by the meanings of their simple constituents, together with syntactic structure, explaining how words and structures get their meaning in effect explains how all expressions get their meaning: a meaning is either a use property (in the case of words and simple structures) or else is determined by these via compositionality.

From this perspective, there is no call to provide a theory of meaning, that is, there is no call to specify meanings, identifying them in such a way that one who knows that an expression has a certain meaning, thus identified, thereby understands it. From Horwich's point of view, this is simply an extraneous project: 'a vital aspect of the deflationary attitude is to question whether there is a need for any such deeper, more immediate characterization of that meaning' (cf. Horwich, 2001, p. 83). If we accept that there is no such need, then we can have compositionality without taking any stand at all about what any meanings *are*, in the sense of how they should be specified in order to reflect what understanding involves. The crucial thesis to be argued for concerns how meanings are 'engendered' (to use the term that quickly becomes standard in Horwich 2001) or 'constituted' (to use the term more commonly used in Horwich 1998): that is, to specify the psychological supervenience base of semantic properties. Deflationism in this regard is in effect the claim that we need not entertain any substantive theories about the understanding-revealing identities or natures of meanings.[4] F&L are too quick to read Horwich's talk of how meanings are 'constituted' (as in the quotation in the first paragraph of this section) as equivalent to talk of what meanings *are*, as this would be understood in the framework of a theory of meaning. For Horwich, this distinction is critical to stating the deflationist project: the deflationist can be properly concerned to state the *constitution* of meanings, that is, to indicate the psychological facts upon which they supervene,

---

[4] There are trivial theories, including statements like '"Mars" means MARS'. The triviality of the 'capitalizing convention' is precisely a manifestation of the deflation of meaning. Another manifestation is Horwich's sympathetic treatment of translational accounts of meaning: these do not specify meanings as such, but pair translations (cf. Horwich, *op. cit.* 2001, p. 82).

but not to state what they *are*, that is, to specify them in the manner of a theory of meaning, a theory knowledge of which would suffice for understanding. (Since either of these ambitions could be characterized as saying what meanings are, there is considerable potential for confusion.)

Horwich's views about meaning are highly controversial, but the present point is simply that merely affirming that meanings should be specified in a theory of meaning would not be dialectically appropriate; nor would any view which presupposes this need. Yet this is what I find in F&L: in keeping with what can fairly be called the dominant view, they take it for granted that meanings need to be specified, as in a theory of meaning. When compositionality is added to this presupposition it certainly delivers constraints on what lexical meanings can be, that is, on how lexical meanings should be specified for meaning-theoretic purposes, just as F&L say. But their breath is likely to be wasted against Horwich, who explicitly rejects the presupposition.

This characterization of their disagreement is supported by their dispute about the Uniformity Assumption. Horwich characterizes it as follows:

> If the meanings of words are engendered by their G-properties, then so are the meanings of complexes. (Horwich 2001, p. 88)

As Horwich says, it is central to his position to deny this. For him, the meanings of words are *engendered* by their use, whereas the meanings of complexes are engendered by the meanings of words: non-uniformity is built in. F&L describe the 'Uniformity Thesis' (*sic*) rather differently, as follows:

> if the meanings of the primitives are stereotypes (or uses, or prototypes, or inferential roles, or whatever), then the meanings of the complexes are *also* stereotypes (or uses, or prototypes, or inferential roles, etc.). (Fodor and Lepore, 2001, p. 73)

Though Horwich is committed to denying this also, he denies it not because of the assumption of uniformity it contains, but because of the assumption that it is important to say what meanings *are*, in the understanding-revealing way. F&L take this importance for granted, whereas Horwich is concerned with what engenders meanings. They assume that meanings need to be identified (as stereotypes or whatever) and this is what Horwich denies. The parties take opposing views, but there is no real dialectic.

3. Compound meanings vs finite semantics

A standard formulation of compositionality is as follows:

> The meaning of a compound expression is a function of the meaning of its parts. (Janssen 1997, p. 419)

In other words, there is a function which, given the meaning of a compound's parts as argument, delivers the compound's meaning as value. Taken literally, a function's values and arguments need to be entities. But such formulations invite a less literal interpretation, which avoids the need for meanings as entities: there is a rule which leads from what the parts of a compound mean to what the compound itself means. I suggest that a weaker formulation of this kind is all that a reasonable thesis of compositionality ought to demand, and that it can be met by familiar semantic theories which could properly be deemed not to meet stronger demands in terms of functions.

F&L (2001) are willing to advance from the early formulation in terms of the meanings of compounds being 'constructed from' the meanings of their components to the claim that the compound meanings have the simpler meanings as parts. They suggest that this explains the relevant supervenience relations between understanding complexes and understanding their parts. The explanatory power of this bold metaphysics is doubtful: even if the properties of a whole supervene on the properties of its parts, it doesn't follow that there is a corresponding supervenience of understanding. Understanding of the relevant kind is knowing how to use correctly, but one might understand a whole, a car for example, that is, know how to use it correctly, without in any sense understanding its parts; or one might understand the parts of a whole, for example a watch, without understanding that a watch is for telling the time.

One ground for suspicion of meanings is that they do not link to understanding in a suitable way. To understand an expression is to know what it means. If meanings are entities, it is natural to read this as knowing the relevant entity. But as all are agreed, and as Horwich stresses, one could know the entity without understanding the expression.[5] If meanings are entities, understanding

---

[5] 'it cannot be my *explicit* knowledge of this fact [that "Mars rotates" means MARS ROTATES] that constitutes my understanding of the sentence; for that would be too easy; I can explicitly infer it from the capitalising convention for naming meanings' (Horwich, *op. cit.* 2001, p. 91). So knowing a meaning may not be enough for understanding: not if

an expression involves not just knowing which entity is its meaning, but also identifying the entity in an appropriate way. Everything that matters to understanding will thus move away from the nature of the supposed entity and towards ways of thinking about the entity: the supposed entities become insignificant to the theory.[6]

Traditionally the main explanandum for compositionality has been linguistic novelty or creativity, something mentioned by Frege,[7] and stressed by Wittgenstein in the *Tractatus*:

> 4.027 It belongs to the essence of a proposition that it should be able to communicate a *new* sense to us.
>
> 4.03 A proposition must use old expressions to communicate a new sense.

This much is delivered by the truism, without engagement with the view that meanings are entities. But there is room for a more ambitious thesis. The truism's 'thanks to' does not say that understanding words and arrangements is sufficient for understanding the wholes they compose. But if the meanings of the wholes is to be 'a function of' the meanings of their parts, we should be able to derive facts about what compounds mean from facts about what their parts mean. This is a standard aim of semantic theory, whether Davidson's truth-theoretic semantics or Montague grammar. It is an aim which can be achieved even when an analogous thesis relating to meanings as entities fails. For example, Tarski-style accounts of quantification meet the aim of deriving what compounds containing quantifiers mean from facts about what their parts mean. But if meanings are entities assigned by models on an interpretation, standard accounts do not meet the condition of making the meaning of a whole a function of the meaning of its parts: on an interpretation, the meaning of a variable is an entity and the meaning of a sentence is a truth value, but there is

---

the meaning is identified merely by the operation of the capitalising convention. Even the greatest enthusiasts for Horwich's position would have to allow, as F&L imply, that his attempt to finesse this problem in terms of implicit knowledge leaves some unanswered questions.

[6] This argument is elaborated by Sainsbury 2001.

[7] Frege 1923, p. 55: 'It is astonishing what language can do. With a few syllables it can express an incalculable number of thoughts, so that even a thought grasped by a terrestrial being for the very first time can be put into a form of words which will be understood by someone to whom the thought is entirely new. This would be impossible, were we not able to distinguish parts in the thoughts corresponding to the parts of a sentence, so that the structure of the sentence serves as an image of the structure of the thoughts.'

no function from the first (plus the other meanings in a sentence) to the second, for the interpretation of a quantification needs also to look at *other* interpretations, ones on which the variable is assigned *other* entities (cf. Janssen 1997, p. 422). The aim of providing a derivation of what wholes mean from what their parts mean is all that will be meant by compositionality in what follows, and this thesis is not committed to meanings as entities.

4. Understanding utterances: pragmatic ambiguity as a resource for compositionalists

Compositionality is a more challenging principle when extended from sentences to utterances. The truism still holds: one understands utterances thanks to understanding the words used in making them; but indexicality shows that other cognitive resources are involved as well. For example, one must use general cognitive skills to identify the referent of a use of a demonstrative pronoun like 'that'.

It is not obvious that indexicality dooms principles of compositionality for utterances. A defence might be constructed by focusing on the occasion-specific meanings of words.[8] Perhaps the general meaning of pronouns, used demonstratively, is that they introduce a rule telling one (in greater or less detail) how to determine their referent as uttered on specific occasions. The rule for 'I' is that it is to refer to the speaker of the utterance in which it occurs, and for 'elle' that it is to refer to something of feminine gender made suitably salient in the context. To understand an utterance containing a demonstratively used pronoun involves knowing the relevant general rule *and* applying it in the specific context. This conception of understanding seems to compose: one understands an utterance of 'Elle a faim' if one uses the rule for 'elle' to come to know to whom or what it refers on the occasion, and appreciates that that entity has been said to be hungry.

One could count indexicality as a species of 'pragmatic ambiguity', on the grounds that a sentence containing an indexical may be used to say different things on different occasions, as a

---

[8] For example, one might distinguish, as Kaplan 1977 does, between character (the general meaning of a type of expression) and content (the specific meaning an expression introduces as uttered on an occasion as a function of its character together with the context).

function of context. But because each of the different things said emerges from an understanding of different ways in which a simple expression interacts, by a semantic rule, with the context of its use, it arguably poses no threat to an appropriately formulated thesis of compositionality.

A serious utterance of 'It's raining' is normally (perhaps always) taken to say that it's raining at some particular place and some particular time. The temporal element can be classified with 'I' and 'elle' as a manifestation of overt indexicality: the rule for the present tense says (ignoring such complications as the historic present) that the relevant time is the time of utterance, so understanding the utterance involves understanding it as saying, concerning the time of utterance, that it is raining *then*. But there seems to be no expression which in this way introduces the place of which rain is predicated, so utterances like this appear to be counterexamples to compositionality principles for utterances (cf. Crimmins and Perry 1989).[9]

Although this phenomenon can be treated in more than one way, the response I need to highlight for the subsequent discussion is that of attributing *covert indexicality*. On this view, at some level of description of the sentence (its 'logical form'), there is an implicit variable for places, and understanding an utterance of the sentence requires the understander to identify the appropriate place (cf. Stanley 2000). If indexicality in general is consistent with compositionality for utterances, then so is covert indexicality.

By contrast, the distinction between referential and attributive uses of definite descriptions as a pragmatically determined difference in truth conditions arguably does pose a threat to compositionality. The idea is that in some description sentences there is no lexical or structural ambiguity, but proper understanding of an utterance of one involves selecting one or other truth condition, the singular truth condition appropriate to the referential reading, or the existentially general truth condition appropriate to the attributive, and that this is to be done on a holistic contextual basis.[10] This

---

[9] 'Our semantics is not compositional, but there is system in the noncompositional mayhem' (Crimmins and Perry 1989, p. 711). Systematicity is their substitute for compositionality. In fact, on their view it would seem that *propositions* are compositional, even if sentences are not.

[10] Presentations of the referential/attributive distinction as this kind of pragmatic ambiguity are given by, for example, Stalnaker 1970, pp. 41–3, Recanati 1993, pp. 282–3, and Bezuidenhout 1997. Recanati makes a good case for this having been Donnellan's original intention, though one misunderstood by many commentators. A compositionalist who accepts Donnellan's data about the truth values of utterances containing definite descriptions will see this as evidence for lexical ambiguity: cf. Evans 1982, p. 325.

selection is not based upon an understanding of any part of the utterance but is required for understanding. So understanding the whole goes beyond an understanding of the parts. The compositionalist, therefore, cannot accept every form of pragmatic ambiguity as consistent with his thesis. There certainly are several alternative ways in which various kinds of pragmatic ambiguity can be accommodated within a compositionalist viewpoint. I will take covert indexicality as my example, though what I shall suggest for most of the cases I wish to discuss is that it is wrong to treat the allegedly ambiguous examples as ambiguous at all. If this is right, the compositionalist has no case to answer.

5. Apparent counterexamples to compositionality

In the following examples, the compounds are supposed to be ambiguous, while their parts and manner of construction have no relevant ambiguity. The conclusion is supposed to be that their meaning (any one of the various meanings they ambiguously possess) goes beyond the meaning of the parts, so that they are counterexamples to compositionality: the semantic properties of such compounds could not be assigned by a theorem derived from axioms assigning semantic properties to its constituents. (The examples are consistent with the truism, since even in such cases understanding the words plays some part in understanding the compound, enough to justify 'thanks to'.)

1. adjectival modification:
   (a) 'Italian book': book in Italian, book about Italy, book made in Italy, book in the pile to take to Italy?[11]
   (b) 'feline care': care for, by, of or in the manner of felines?
2. genitives:
   (a) 'John's leg': one (which?) of the limbs composing John's body, or the leg which John, a student of anatomy, is dissecting?
   (b) 'John's table': the/a table John owns, has sold, has bought, has borrowed, has lent, wants to use, often uses, made, . . .?
3. compounded nouns:
   (a) 'sand cleaner': something which cleans sand or which uses sand to clean?

[11] Perhaps 'Italian' is both noun (denoting a language or a native of Italy) and adjective. These examples are supposed to keep to the adjectival form, though ambiguity about which form is at issue can arise.

(b) 'hi-tec management': management of a business producing or servicing hi-tec things, or management by methods involving hi-tec?
4. noun + verb
   (a) 'John runs': with his legs? Or like butter runs when hot, or paint runs when wet, or like the Thames runs from Oxford to London?
   (b) 'John smokes': cigarettes? or emits smoke (like Etna)?
5. the Travis effect:
   (a) 'Those leaves are green', when brown leaves are painted green, may mean something false (if we are interested in natural colour as a sign of something) or something true (if we are merely interested in chromatic matters).
   (b) 'The squash ball is round' may mean something true (as round is its normal shape) or something false (as it is currently in violent contact with the wall and so nearly hemispherical).

In each case, there are supposed to be two or more 'readings' or 'disambiguations' corresponding to different meanings. But the parts are not relevantly ambiguous, and there is no relevant ambiguity in how they are put together. Hence the various meanings are not determined by the meaning of the parts and how they are combined. Hence a semantic theory could not derive suitable properties for the compounds from suitable properties for their parts.

Taking it for granted that the anti-compositionalist objector is right to say that there is no relevant lexical or structural ambiguity, a defender of compositionality in the face of the counterexamples has various options, and I shall consider just two of them.

6. Covert indexicality. Some alleged counterexamples display not ambiguity but different assignments to hidden indexical elements.
7. Unspecific meaning. The counterexamples confuse distinct 'readings', that is, distinct meanings, with distinct ways in which one and the same meaning could be true.[12]

---

[12] This option has been applied to alleged ambiguities in sentences with more than one quantifier by, among others, Kempson and Cormack (1981). If their word 'interpretation' can be read as 'way of being true', their §6 provides a well-argued case for the kind of position I am applying to the different cases discussed here.

The drift of this paper is that option (7) has been given insufficient attention, and that it is a good option to take with respect to most of the examples under consideration here. The main argument for favouring (7) is that alternative approaches along the lines of (6) require the determination of a value for the variable if understanding is to be possible, and this does not seem to accord with the facts. This establishes at best that (7) is sometimes the best strategy for the compositionalist, but it does not speak to other cases, and does not address the question whether we are somehow committed to finding some successful compositionalist strategy.

6. Applying the strategies

6.1 Adjectival modification

The objector seems to me right to present cases like (1a) and (1b) as ones in which it is very implausible to attribute either lexical or structural ambiguity. First, there are apparently endless ways in which something can count as an Italian book, not all of which could be foreseen in advance in learning 'Italian' or 'book' or the construction of adjectival modification. If the word is learnt in a context in which the learner appreciates that the contextually salient way for something to be Italian is to be made in Italy, then an ambiguity account would suggest that this is the meaning learnt. It would then be hard to explain the ease with which people go on to use 'Italian' in contexts in which other ways of being Italian are salient. Second, if these cases were to be explained by lexical or structural ambiguity, the ambiguity should be available in cases in which it plainly is not. For example, if there were some fixed meaning of the construction which relates what 'book' refers to with an intended trip to the place referred to by the noun ('Italy') which corresponds to the adjective, then 'generous book' should have a reading (although perhaps one hard to access in normal contexts) on which it refers to a book in the pile to take to generosity. This is not a hard to access reading, but an absurdity.

If these cases are genuinely ambiguous, the ambiguity is pragmatic, as opposed to lexical or structural. In most contexts hearers will identify the intended relation between 'Italian' and 'book'; the identification will draw on context, and will exploit considerations of plausibility and relevance. In the present discussion, the question is whether pragmatic ambiguity arising from covert indexicality can provide an adequate account.

On the covert indexical theory, the logical form of 'Italian book' could be represented by something like 'Italian R book', where the interpretation of the relation variable R is to be supplied by the context. The form 'x R y' could be interpreted so as to be true of the satisfiers of y which are written in a language which satisfies x, or so as to be true of the satisfiers of y manufactured in a place which satisfies the noun from which x is formed, and so on. The account has the advantage over accounts in terms of lexical or structural ambiguity of not requiring that the various readings of the construction be settled in advance. Moreover, context can point to sensible interpretations of R, and can place obstacles in the way of accessing interpretations which, in other contexts, would be natural. However, unless nothing better can be found, it seems an extraordinary account as applied to this kind of case. It implies that you would not have understood an utterance like 'Let's read an Italian book together' unless you had identified such an R; whereas in fact it seems you do understand even when you are in doubt about R. True, you may go on to ask 'Do you mean a book in Italian or a book about Italy?', but this no more shows that you did not understand the first remark than if, in response to 'Let's go to the movies' you say 'Do you mean let's go tonight or later?'. In both cases, the proposal was fully intelligible but not fully specific.

Another difficulty for the covert indexical account is that once context has made one determination of the variable salient, it should remain salient throughout the sentence unless there are contrary indications, and a shift would produce a special zeugmatic effect. For example, it would be odd to say

8. It's foggy; cold too

in the hope that context would determine different places for fog and cold, making (8) in effect equivalent to:

9. It's foggy – here in London; cold too – there in Iceland.

However, there's at least no firm intuition that there is something odd about the following shift:

10. This is an Italian book – it's by Ginzburg; and this is another Italian one – it's in the Lonely Planet series and has lots of information about Italy.

An alternative to the covert indexicality account is to say that 'Italian' functions just as one would expect from a dictionary entry: 'Italian *F*' is satisfied by a satisfier of *F* of or pertaining to Italy. This is an unspecific but definite, unambiguous and complete meaning. An Italian book is one of or pertaining to Italy, and a book may pertain to Italy by being on my pile of books to take there, or by being about Italy, or by being manufactured in Italy, or by being written in the dominant language of Italy. The different so-called readings of a sentence like 'Let's read an Italian book' do not correspond to different senses or meanings, but to different ways in which 'we read an Italian book' can be made true: by reading a book written in Italian or a book about Italy or a book from my pile of books to take to Italy. It is no more correct to regard this as ambiguity than to regard 'John runs' as ambiguous on the grounds that it could be made true by John running in bare feet or in trainers, quickly or slowly, east or west.

It seems to me hard to deny (a) that we should distinguish different 'readings' of a sentence from different ways in which it could be made true and (b) that this distinction has not always been scrupulously adhered to. There is plenty of scope for detailed disagreement about precisely how the distinction divides the cases. In order to promote the claims of unspecific but determinate and unambiguous meanings, I will show, quickly and rather dogmatically, how the idea applies to various other cases.

'Feline care' is satisfied, in the same sense though not in the same way, by a vet tending a cat and by a cat tending the puppy to which is she acting as foster mother. Both vet and cat supply care of or pertaining to felines, the vet by supplying care for a feline, the cat by being a feline which supplies care.

6.2 Genitives

I claim these are similar: their meanings are highly unspecific, and cover a range of cases. John's leg or table is a leg or table of or pertaining to John, which a leg or table may be in various ways. There are many different ways in which 'John's leg is on his table' may be true, but the different ways are ways in which the same meaning can be true.

Here is an argument for an alternative account in terms of covert indexicality:

Understanding a singular noun phrase like 'John's table' involves identifying the object to which it refers, but one cannot do this until one knows what relation is supposed to link John to a table. The alleged unspecific meaning is not something that can be understood. On the covert indexicality theory, however, a full understanding requires that the relevant relation be identified, and this will lead to the identification of the relevant object, and without this identification the utterance cannot be understood.

The first premise is questionable. Perhaps one identifies something only by connecting it with antecedently possessed singular information relating to it. In that case, identification is not a prerequisite for understanding: definite descriptions can be understood even if they fail to denote, or if they do denote but the denoted object is unfamiliar to the understander. If the relevant notion of identification is weakened, perhaps to 'one identifies an object, as the supposed referent of a noun phrase, only if one can give a satisfactory answer to the question "to which object was the speaker, by using that phrase, purporting to refer?" ' then it is unclear that a non-parrot-like repetition of 'John's table' is an unsatisfactory answer. If the standards of what is satisfactory are raised, genuine cases of understanding will be misclassified as cases in which there is no understanding.

A further consideration favouring unspecific meaning over covert indexicality is that one can mix different possessive relations without incongruity:

11. This is indeed my book [sc. the one I wrote], but it's yours now [sc. belongs to you].[13]

6.3 Compounded nouns

On the unspecific account, the determinate meaning does not supply specific information about how the satisfiers of the nouns are related. If we know that a carpet cleaner cleans carpets whereas a vacuum cleaner cleans using a (partial) vacuum, or that traffic lights control rather than illuminate traffic, or that a band saw does not saw bands but saws with a band, this is not semantic knowledge, but non-semantic knowledge, concerning cleaners, traffic and saws, knowledge of which of the ways for an unspecific content to be true is most likely to be in question. No doubt there are or could be traffic lights which illuminate traffic, cleaning machines which use carpets as flails to clean, and saws designed specially for sawing bands.

In defence of this approach, consider a more complex case. A chemical purifier factory may be a factory that makes chemical purifiers, or one that uses chemical purifiers in making something

---

[13] There is also a shift from type to token.

else. Each of these two possibilities divides into two, for a chemical purifier may purify a chemical or purify by using a chemical. So there are (at least) four possibilities for chemical purifier factories. On a covert indexical view of compounded nouns, a context in which 'A chemical purifier factory is to be built at the end of your garden' is intelligible is one which selects just one out of (a minimum of) four possibilities, and understanding the utterance involves knowing which was selected. This seems a highly implausible view. Once you learn that a chemical purifier factory is to be built at the end of your garden, you know enough to start making a fuss and writing to your MP without needing to know exactly what form the horror will take. Unspecific meaning seems just the right account.

Suppose that context somehow makes salient the pair of relations <using, making>, so that a contextual determination view would say that an utterance of 'A chemical purifier factory is to be built at the end of your garden' in that context is true iff a factory which makes things which are used to purify a chemical is to be built at the end of your garden. Suppose that in fact what is to be built at the end of your garden is a factory which makes things which purify by using a chemical. It seems to me nonetheless true that a chemical purifier factory is to be built at the end of your garden; this is inconsistent with a covert indexical account.

6.4 Verbs

There probably is a transitive/non-transitive ambiguity in many verbs, including 'runs' and 'smokes'. Within non-transitive running, there are many kinds, as illustrated in (4a). Many will typically be hard to access in a context. Perhaps some ways are excluded by restrictions relating to semantic categories. But we should not be too swift to think we know the exclusions. A recent cost-reducing innovation in the undertaking business involves chemically liquefying the corpses and running them into the public drains. John, once dead and in the grip of the innovators, can run like warm butter. There is no need to recognize semantic (as opposed to business) innovation here, or any change of meaning.

(4b) illustrates transitive/non-transitive ambiguity in 'smokes', and so does not as such pose a threat to the compositionalist. Within the transitive use it is surprising how unspecific the meaning turns out to be, as the following puzzle illustrates: how can a cigarette be half-smoked without being shorter than before? To smoke a cigarette you normally put one end in your mouth, light the other, and puff. To smoke a salmon, you normally soak it in brine for one and a half hours, hang it in your chimney, and when it is dry light little piles of oak chips at the bottom of the chimney and leave it for eight hours. There are different ways of smoking, but no ambiguity in the word 'smoke'. You *could* smoke a cigarette by soaking it in brine for one and a half hours, hanging it in your chimney, and when it is dry lighting little piles of oak chips at the bottom of the chimney. Then half-smoking a cigarette, smoking it for a mere four hours, may not shrink it much or at all. This way of smoking cigarettes is much better for your health than the normal one. Trying to smoke a salmon in the way cigarettes are usually smoked is unlikely to be successful; but one understands what it would be to try this, and this suggests that there is no relevant ambiguity in 'smoke'.

6.5 The Travis effect

This can suggest some radical conclusions about the nature of language, of which failure of compositionality is at the conservative end of the spectrum. I believe that at least some of these cases can be dealt with by seeing meanings as suitably unspecific, though other cases are best described in terms of covert indexicality (and perhaps yet other cases are genuine counterexamples to compositionality). I start by elaborating the examples a little.[14]

(5a) 'Those leaves are green.' Brown leaves have been painted green. Suppose we are part of a commission inspecting Vietnam to determine whether Pentagon denials that it has used defoliants are true. Brown leaves are signs of the early stages of the action of defoliants. Travis suggests that, in this context, the truth about the painted leaves is that they are not green. The sentence has a meaning such that the facts just described make it false. Now suppose that we are trying to select camouflage material. Only green things will do, and more or less anything green will do. In this context, Travis suggests, the truth about the very same leaves is that they are green. The sentence has a meaning such that the same leaf-related facts make it false. Yet the sentence is not ambiguous, so it has only one meaning, it relates only to the leaves and the leaves are in the same state in both circumstances.

---

[14] Sources are Travis (1985, 1994, 1996). Travis (1994) in effect denies compositionality for utterances or thoughts, on the grounds that many pragmatic determinations operate differently from those at work in determining reference for indexicals.

This seems like a contradiction. Travis avoids it by denying that there is a proper conception of meaning which determines the truth conditions of what is said on an occasion (even allowing for the kind of context sensitivity manifested by pronouns).

I suggest that 'Those leaves are green' is true in both cases, but that in the first a participant who came to learn that it is true would jump to the conclusion that it is made true in the normal way, rather than the exceptional way. This participant would be led astray; but one can easily be led astray by the truth (as by Desdemona's handkerchief). The meaning of 'green' is unspecific: there must be a green surface, but the meaning is indifferent to how deep the colour runs and how the surface got to be that colour. We generally make normal assumptions about these things, just as we assume that 'John smokes' is true in virtue of John smoking cigarettes or cigars or a pipe, rather than in virtue of frequently smoking salmon. But we have no difficulty in seeing that these normal assumptions may fail to hold.

(5b) 'The ball is round.' A first time spectator at a squash game asks if the ball is round. He wants to know whether squash resembles soccer, in being played with a round ball, or rugger, in being played with a ball which is not round. The right answer to the question is 'Yes', even if the ball is currently far from round thanks to having been hit against the wall.

In a contrasting case, a manufacturer of squash balls is trying out a new material. For the trials, tiny transmitters have been inserted into the skin of the ball to measure reactions to deformations. The instrument adjacent to the court, which is supposed to register the signals, is flat, which is as it should be if the ball is not at that moment deformed. The technician asks if the ball is round. If the ball is at that point ovoid through being against the wall, the right answer is 'No'.

In these cases, I find it hard not to accept Travis's judgements of truth value, and this marks a difference from the other cases we have considered. For example, it was claimed that 'Italian book' is ambiguous; but it was not explicitly claimed that 'That's an Italian book' could be both true and false of the same book, depending on which meaning is selected in the context. Had this claim been made, I would have rejected it.[15] But in the present

---

[15] One can hear an utterance of these words as both true and false if one supplies different implicit qualifications, but such a case is merely like 'Clinton is good (as a statesman) and not good (as a husband)'.

case I find myself compelled to agree that 'The ball is round' is
made both true and false by the same ball in the same condition,
depending on the context. This rules out the account in terms of
unspecific meaning, for within the classical perspective which I
accept, but which Travis is trying to undermine, utterances with a
single meaning, however unspecific, cannot be made to have
opposite truth values by the same facts.

This leaves three options: either this example is of a failure of
compositionality, or there is some lexical or structural ambiguity
we have not yet considered, or there is a hidden contextual variable taking different values in the different cases.

Perhaps the present tense introduces a covert indexical for a
stretch of time. An utterance containing 'is ϕ' has as logical form
'is ϕ for at least t' where the variable over temporal intervals is
contextually determined (or determined in part by context and
in part by the semantic character of ϕ). Polar values for this variable are *at this very moment*, and *in a general way*. John is writhing
in the dentist's chair. Is he happy? Not right now; but he is in a
general way. Each of these values is probably also vague.

The two squash ball utterances pick up different values for t as
a function in part of the concerns and interests of the participants. Hence the interpreted utterances say different things; and
so, by one standard, differ in meaning. There is no counterexample to compositionality, any more than there is (or so we are
supposing for the sake of the present discussion) in the fact that
'Elle a faim' can be used to say different things.

7. Conclusion

While it can hardly be doubted that some measure of compositionality of understanding of utterances obtains, there is no apriori guarantee that it is universal. Even the staunchest defenders of
compositionality admit this in their recognition of 'idiom': you
cannot derive the standard colloquial meaning of 'kicked the
bucket' from a proper specification of the meaning of its parts. So
we are left with a somewhat messy question: how far do these fail-
ures extend? In this paper I have considered some reasonably
common *kinds* of apparent failure: locutions widespread enough
that if compositionality failed for them, the claimed general
compositionality for English would require serious qualification.

The counterexamples have taken the form of expressions
which allegedly have different meanings or readings, even though

there is no relevant lexical or structural ambiguity among their parts. In most cases, there are very many ways in which utterances containing the expressions could be true, and sometimes there seems no way of containing or listing all possibilities in advance. This tends to reduce the attractiveness of attempts to find some hidden lexical or structural ambiguity, for lexical and structural meanings must be fixed and potentially known in advance. Approaches in terms of covert indexicality provide an appropriate kind of flexibility, but they suffer the defect that they predict that an utterance cannot be understood unless a specific value is assigned to the hidden variable, and in many cases this seems at variance with the facts. The claim that meaning is often unspecific deals well with a number of cases, though it cannot handle ones in which we are convinced that the utterances of the same sentence with the same reference for all explicit elements can have opposite truth values, as a function of context. In such cases, the most plausible option for the compositionalist, unless ambiguity can be detected in the components, is a covert indexicality view.

Horwich and F&L disagreed about the implications of compositionality, but not about its reality. I have argued that its reality should not be taken for granted, and that the extent to which our language is compositional is not to be decided by general apriori reasoning, but by detailed examination of specific cases.[16]

King's College London
London WC2R 2LS
UK
mark.sainsbury@kcl.ac.uk

References

Bezuidenhout, A. (1997). 'Pragmatics, semantic underdetermination and the referential/attributive distinction.' *Mind* 106, 375–409.
Crimmins, M. and J. Perry (1989). 'The prince and the phone booth.' *Journal of Philosophy* 86, 685–711.
Evans, G. (1982). *The Varieties of Reference.* Oxford: Clarendon Press.
Fodor, J. and E. Lepore (2001). 'Why compositionality won't go away: reflections on Horwich's 'deflationary' theory.' *Ratio* 14, 350–368. Reprinted in this volume: ch. 5, 58–76.
Frege, G. (1884). *Die Grundlagen der Arithmetik.* Breslau.
Frege, G. (1923). 'Compound thoughts.' In Geach, P. T. and R. H. Stoothof (trans.) *Logical Investigations.* Oxford: Basil Blackwell, 55–78.

[16] Thanks to Ruth Kempson for discussion of these issues and to the Leverhulme Trust for a Senior Research Fellowship during the tenure of which this paper was written.

114   R.M. SAINSBURY

Horwich, P. (1998). *Meaning*. Oxford: Oxford University Press.
Horwich, P. (2001). 'Deflating compositionality.' *Ratio* 14, 369–85. Reprinted in this volume: Ch. 6, 77–93.
Janssen, T.M.V. (1997) 'Compositionality.' In Benthem, J. van and A. ter Meulen, eds, *Handbook of Logic and Language*. Amsterdam: Elsevier, 417–474.
Kaplan, D. (1977). 'Demonstratives.' Reprinted in Almog, J., J. Perry and H. Wettstein, eds, (1989) *Themes from Kaplan*. Oxford: Oxford University Press, 481–614.
Kempson, R.M and A. Cormack (1981). 'Ambiguity and quantification.' *Linguistics and Philosophy* 4, 259–309.
Récanati, F. (1993.) *Direct Reference*. Oxford: Blackwell Publishers.
Sainsbury, R.M. (2001). 'Knowing meanings and knowing entities.' In Meixner, U. and P. Simons, eds, *Metaphysics in the Post-Metaphysical Age: Proceedings of the 22nd International Wittgenstein Symposium, 1999*, 106–115.
Stalnaker, R. (1970). 'Pragmatics.' *Synthese*. Reprinted in his (1999) *Context and Content*. Oxford: Oxford University Press, 31–46.
Stalnaker, R. (1997). 'Reference and necessity.' In Hale, B. and C. Wright, eds, *A Companion to the Philosophy of Language*. Oxford: Blackwell, 534–554.
Stanley, J. (2000). 'Context and logical form.' *Linguistics and Philosophy* 23, 391–434.
Travis, C. (1985). 'On what is strictly speaking true.' *Canadian Journal of Philosophy* 15, 187–229.
Travis, C. (1994). 'On Constraints of Generality.' *Proceedings of the Aristotelian Society* 94, 165–88.
Travis, C. (1996). 'Meaning's role in truth.' *Mind* 105, 451–466.
Wittgenstein, L. (1921). *Tractatus Logico-Philosophicus*. London: Routledge and Kegan Paul.

INDEX

116

INDEX

God 39–40, 45
grammar 19, 21, 50–1
 Montague grammar 100
Grice, P 13

hallucinations 45
 veridical 34, 39
Harman, G 45–6
Hornsby, J 13, 13n 15
Horwich, P 2–4, 58, 94–9, 113
Husserl, E 50

Ideas 26, 29, 32
identification of objects 83, 108
idiolect 7n 65, 91
idiom 60, 71, 76, 95, 112
implicit belief – see belief
indexicality 101–2
 covert 94, 102–7, 109, 112–3
inference 32, 62–4, 66–8, 71, 76, 79, 80, 85, 19n 91, 92
 inferential role semantics – see use theory of meaning
intensionality 51
intentional fallacy 63
intentionality 25, 27–8, 30, 52
 intentional objects 1, 26, 43–4, 47, 49, 51–3, 55–6
 intentional properties 38–40
interpretation 26, 29–30, 77, 81–2, 101, 12n 104. See also translation manuals
Italian 77, 81, 103, 105–7, 111

Janssen, T 99, 101

knowledge
 of meaning 62–3, 67, 82, 84–5
 implicit vs. explicit – see beliefs
Kripke, S 19

language of thought 27, 53, 65, 68–70, 75–6, 82, 87, 92–3
law-like correlation 28
Lewis, D 13, 16–7, 19
lexical items 3
lexical meaning 59, 70–5, 17n 90
lexicon 61–2, 71
logical equivalence 18n 22
logical form 4, 69–70, 75–6, 79, 102, 106
Luria, A.R 50

meanings (see also content; representation)
 as entities 94–5, 99–100

unspecific 94, 104, 107, 109–111, 113
mental
 processes 28, 53, 66, 69–70
 representations 27–8, 69
Mentalese – see language of thought
metaphysics 43–4, 50, 58, 6n 63, 64, 66
 of belief 65
 of meaning 60, 99
 of mind 26
 of understanding 60
Mill, J.S 6
music 49–50

names – see proper names
natural language 86, 91
neural state 16–17
nominalized sentences 2, 8, 11–13, 18–20, 23
non-existent objects – see objects
noumenal 32, 38, 41
noun phrases 6, 11, 14–5, 19, 104
 compounded 103, 108–9
 singular 107
 verbal and deverbal 5–6, 8, 10–13
number 83

objects
 non-existent 44–7, 49, 54–6
 of experience 48, 51
 of thought – see intentionality
 physical objects 31, 44, 47–9, 51
 vague objects 46–7
occurent understanding – see belief
ontology 25, 29–31, 33, 44, 48–9, 51

pain 16–8
paraphrase 11, 13
perception 5–6, 13–6, 41, 45
poverty of stimulus argument 75
pragmatic ambiguity – see ambiguity
predicate logic 79–81, 86
Price, H.H 45
primitive expressions – see expressions
proper names 6–7, 78
propositions 20, 48, 54, 72, 95
Putnam, H 26, 29, 33

quantification 46, 100–1, 12n 104
Quine, W.V.O 46, 77, 2n 78

reference 72, 78, 85, 108
regress argument 68–70
relations 11–13, 16, 18–9
 causal – see causal relations
 cognitive 16–18
 real vs. nominal 5–6

Printed and bound by CPI Group (UK) Ltd, Croydon, CR0 4YY

09/06/2025

14686103-0002